AF207590

Mr. Celebrity

The Autobiography of Earl Blackwell

Written by
Earl Blackwell
with
Patsy Maharam

Photographs are from the author's collection (except where noted)

Every reasonable effort has been made to trace the ownership of photos included in this volume. Any errors which may have occurred are inadvertent and will be corrected in subsequent editions, provided notification is sent to the publisher.

Requests for permission to make copies of any part of the work should be mailed to:
Permissions Dept., C.I.P.R., 171 West 57th Street, NYC, NY 10019

Library of Congress Catologing-in-Publication Data
Blackwell, Earl, 1913 -
Mr. Celebrity (The autobiography of Earl Blackwell)
by Earl Blackwell with Patsy Maharam

ISBN 0-9631364-0-2

Designed & Printed by Jeff Martin/MCUSA

Printed in the United States of America
First Edition

Mr. Celebrity

The Autobiography of Earl Blackwell

For Vera & Eddy,
with all good wishes,

Earl Blackwell

C.I.P.R., LTD.
171 West 57th Street
New York City, N.Y. 10019

THE ONE

– ii –

When a very young man, admittedly fresh out of Georgia, with a readily identifiable accent and a broad smile, came to lunch by invitation of my wife, Joan Crawford, I had no reason to suspect it was the beginning of a friendship that would last over half a century.

It is always difficult to find someone who is equally at home in the world of theaters as in the world of international "society." Earl Blackwell is one of those rare people. I remember attending a great Costume Ball in Venice which he had organized. While dining first at a dinner given by the well-known hostess Countess Volpi, I looked around the room and noted Mrs. Joseph P. Kennedy, Princess Grace of Monaco, Aristotle Onassis and other world-famous figures brought together by the ubiquitous Earl Blackwell. It was then that I first observed the way he had taken a mere idea for a kind of information bureau on celebrities and proceeded to create a highly original and very international business.

Earl Blackwell's enthusiasm is contagious. As from time to time, he leapt forward with new projects; his unsurpassed energy ensured an important social event. All one had to do was toss Earl the ball and he headed for the touchdown everytime. His eye for detail is well-known. At the party he gave in honor of Noel Coward's conferred knighthood, he took over Raffles, the very exclusive private dining and dancing club. The club had been decorated by Cecil Beaton with dozens of photographs of celebrities lining the walls. Earl changed them all to feature Noel Coward.

I had become interested in real estate development on a Bahamian island about 20 years ago, that had Jack Nicklaus already living there and a fine 18-hole golf course. There was a big opening event where special guests were invited from all parts of the world. I put Earl on my invitation list. Today, he has a beautiful house on the island and is also founder and president of the well-known Tamboo Club there.

No one I know has more varied and attractive friends than Earl Blackwell. This pictorial cavalcade of his celebrated friends is unique. I'm happy to have been part of all that has occupied Earl's attention over the years. It is an era that will probably never be equalled.

– DOUGLAS FAIRBANKS, JR.

My friend for many, many years
– Douglas Fairbanks, Jr.

For
Earl Blackwell,
Best regards,
Bob Jones
Photo: Leonid Skvirsky, MacMillan

Chapter One

I must have been born with a fascination for fame. I was lucky that in Atlanta even in the days when its population numbered only 300,000 (as compared to today's 3,000,000) there were three major newspapers competing with one another. As a result, as a kid I was reading O.O. McIntyre, Arthur Brisbane, Walter Winchell, Louella Parsons and other syndicated writers about New York and Hollywood. Undoubtedly, they were a great influence on my early life.

Growing up in Atlanta, I caddied for legendary golfer, Bobby Jones. In those days the Metropolitan Opera visited Atlanta each Spring and I gave out programs just so I could hear all the operas and go backstage and meet Lily Pons, Rosa Ponselle, Lawrence Tibbett and Gigli. When I was 12, I read about a roundtrip to New York from Savannah by boat for $50.00 and managed to save enough money parking cars at the baseball stadium for the trip. I told my parents I wanted to visit an aunt, but I was actually eager to see Broadway and visit the Paramount motion picture studio in Astoria which I had read so much about.

Somehow I managed to gain entrance to the studio and watched Gloria Swanson making a silent film. After returning home, the *Atlanta Journal* heard about the young boy's trip and sent a reporter to do a Sunday magazine story. The reporter's name was Peggy Mitchell, who ten years later would be known throughout the world as Margaret Mitchell, author of *Gone With The Wind.*

My father was born in Elberton, Georgia, where the Blackwell family had planted its roots in Georgia clay as far back as 1749, long before the American Revolution. My mother's parents came to America from Italy as teenagers on their honeymoon. They settled in Atlanta shortly after Sherman had almost razed the city during the Civil War.

Today in any history written about Atlanta my maternal grandparents, Mary and John Lagomarsino, figure prominently. It was in their home, adjacent to the Governor's Mansion, that I was born. In those days children were born at home, but my case was a bit unusual in that I was born in the same room and in the same bed in which my mother had been born twenty-four years earlier.

My mother was brought up by a traditionally black mammy and, as her mother died when she was just a small child, she never learned to speak Italian. She was a true Southerner. I was taken by her to a parade when I was quite young. There was a band playing "Dixie" and I remember my mother saying, "Son, whenever you hear that song, you stand up and say 'Hooray! Hooray!' " and I still do.

I had a very happy childhood, surrounded by love. When I was about three years old my parents took me out to Grant Park one Sunday afternoon to visit the zoo. They told me to feed the stork so he would bring me a baby brother or sister, and I answered, "If it is a baby brother

Opposite Page: Bobby Jones
Inset: Margaret Mitchell

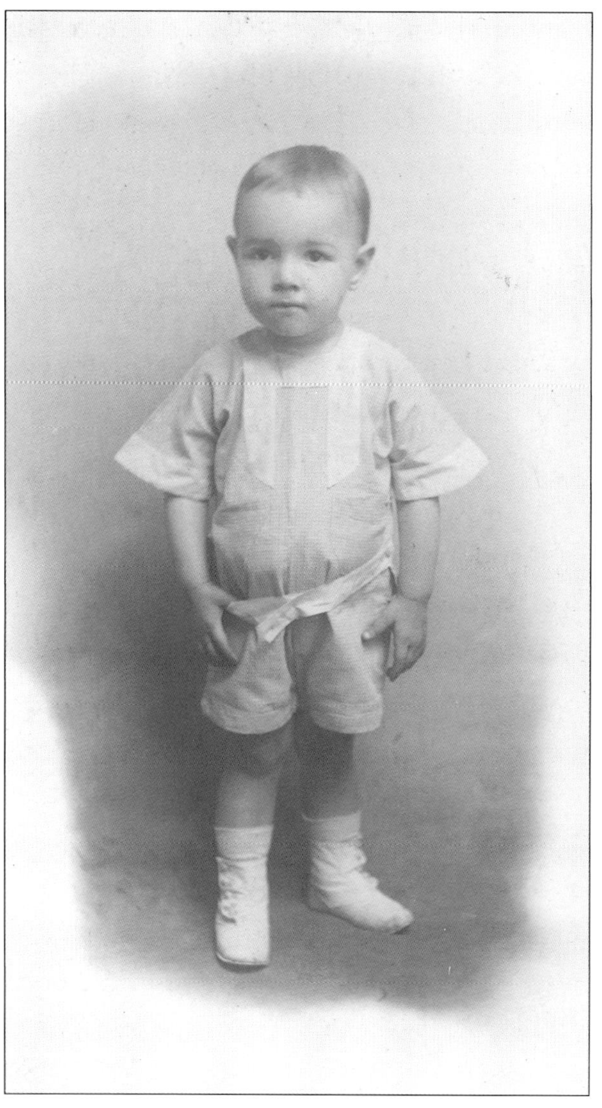

At 3 years old

bedroom and then Aunt Maime came in and whispered "You have a baby sister."

There has been a close bond between my sister and me from that day on. As she grew up and became one of the most popular belles of Atlanta, I would make sure that Mary was home before I was. I knew my mother would be waiting for us, and if I arrived fifteen minutes before my sister, my mother would worry. So many times I would drive around the block to kill time and make sure she was home before me.

I was well aware at a very early age of the intensity of my mother's love. There were times when I was embarrassed and afraid she was showing too much partiality to me, rather than my sister. However, there was no question that she loved Mary with all her heart and gave her all the attention a mother could possibly give a daughter. But there was something special with me. Maybe it was because I was the first born and a boy, but I knew deep down how much she loved me, and I her.

My father's younger sister, Bernice Blackwell, was said to be one of the most beautiful girls in Atlanta. While still in her teens she married a wealthy oral surgeon and moved to Montclair, New Jersey. My Aunt Bernice, having no children, indulged herself with beautiful clothes and jewelry. Then after a short season, she would send evening dresses with Paris labels to Mary. It was always a jubilant day when we arrived home from school and mother announced

I'll give it back. I want a little sister."

A few months later a bassinette appeared in my mother's bedroom and every morning I would run and look into it, eager to see if the stork had brought my baby sister. Then one cold and rainy October evening I remember my wonderful Aunt Maime (she was my mother's older sister) tucked me into bed and kissed me goodnight. A little later, I was awakened by loud cries coming from my mother's

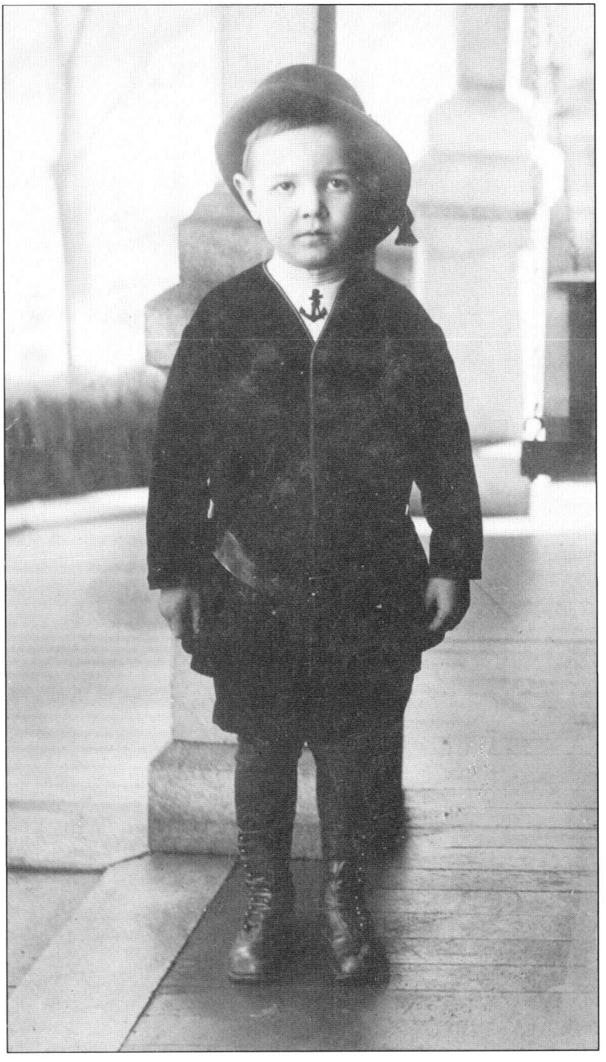

A Southern Gentleman

"A box arrived from Bernice today." Mary and I couldn't wait to see what was waiting for her to wear to the next fraternity dance.

I can't recall my mother or father ever saying "no" to me. I would say "I'm going to be a counselor at Culver Military summer camp in Indiana" and they would say, "What will you need in the way of clothes or uniforms?" or "I've decided to take a bit part in the local stock company" and they would answer "That's nice" or when at 17, I said, "I've decided to go to Columbia

University this summer and take a course in journalism." And I heard … "Then why don't you plan to spend a week with your Aunt Bernice in Montclair before the summer session begins."

I entered Oglethorpe University at the age of 15, not because I was a brilliant student, but circumstances made it possible; Junior High did not exist at the time I graduated from Grammar School. My class was the last one to go directly from the 7th grade into High School and the transition was severe. I can now appreciate the importance of Junior High. In the 7th grade I was still being taught by a gentle female who had known me most of my life and who called me by my first name. Then, to go directly into high school with all boys and a male teacher who called you by your last name was somewhat traumatic. It took a while to adjust, and especially so when I was suddenly faced with Latin and Algebra for the first time.

As I look back, I think the only time of my life that I was not happy and enjoying every minute of every day was the three years I spent at Boys High in Atlanta. Fortunately, my parents decided to spend the winter in Florida my senior year so I was enrolled in the Manatee High School in Bradenton on Florida's West Coast. The Atlanta schools must have been farther advanced in those days because in Florida I found myself going to school at 8:30 A.M. and being dismissed at 10:30 A.M.

Here I am dressed as Charles Ray at the Pi Kappa Phi "Movie Ball" at the East Lake Country Club, Atlanta. I won second prize.

At Christmas time we drove up to Atlanta to spend the Holidays and that's when I asked my parents if it might be possible for me to enter Oglethorpe without finishing my senior year of High School. We went out to the University and I was accepted.

Entering Oglethorpe at an early age was the turning point of my life. In a small university with a student body of one thousand, you could do almost anything you wanted. There wasn't a school paper, so I started one. They were not doing original plays so I wrote and produced a few. The annual musical revue called THE PETREL FOLLIES which I devised is still remembered and talked about in Atlanta today. I would cast the FOLLIES with the most beautiful girls in Atlanta, thereby getting reams of publicity. Also, I would hear of someone like Irving Berlin who was opening a show on Broadway and I would have the nerve to wire him saying, "You're opening your new show on Tuesday evening and my college show opens in Atlanta on Friday, may we use one of your new songs?" Incredibly, they often said, "Sure, go ahead," and I would have banner headlines in the paper the next day.

I remember when John Randolph Hearst entered Oglethorpe. He had just married Dorothy Hart of Los Angeles society and they were still on their honeymoon. I quickly devised a wedding scene for the PETREL FOLLIES and you can imagine who the bride and groom were. Dorothy later married William Paley and after their divorce she married Walter Hirshon.

It was the Summer before my senior year at Oglethorpe that became very special to me. My best friend in college, Almon Raines of Savannah (whose nickname was Nammie) and I had saved enough money to afford a round trip third class ticket to Europe. Before leaving Atlanta, I had stopped by the *Atlanta Constitution* to give them a story, most likely about a fraternity dance or a show I had produced. Being college correspondent to the morning newspaper I contributed stories each week, for which I was paid a small amount for each inch of copy the paper used.

I remember telling the editor's secretary about my approaching European trip and her saying, "Earl, if you run across any good stories in Europe send them back. Wait a minute and I'll give you a letter of introduction."

THE ATLANTA CONSTITUTION

DAILY - SUNDAY - TRI-WEEKLY

ATLANTA, GA.

```
June
14, 1930



To Whom It May Concern:

The bearer of this, Mr. Earl Blackwell, has been
The Constitution's news correspondent at Oglethorpe
University for the past four years.  He is leaving
now for a trip to Europe and incident to his journey
will contribute articles to our columns.

Any courtesy extended to Mr. Blackwell will be appre-
ciated by The Constitution and

Very truly yours,




Assistant to General Manager.
FWC'R
```

My best friend in college Almon 'Nammie" Raines

Nammie and I were booked to sail on the Bremen, which was scheduled to leave at midnight from a pier in Brooklyn. I'll never forget the excitement of that evening. We first went to the Brooklyn Paramount to hear Rudy Vallee, one of my favorite entertainers of that era. Every Thursday evening at eight o'clock I was always glued to the radio to hear the Fleichman Yeast Hour starring Rudy Vallee. One of the reasons I enjoyed this show was because Vallee always introduced the star of a current Broadway musical singing their latest song.

After boarding the ship and finding our cabin (which was located in the lower depths but we didn't mind) we hurried out on deck to see the Statue of Liberty illuminated in all its glory. As the lights of Liberty faded away we started to explore the ship which seemed gigantic. We passed an open bar with people crowding around making toasts to each other. This was the first time I had ever witnessed this, except in the movies. Don't forget it was still prohibition. I recall Nammie and I decided to step up to the bar to celebrate with the others, but for the life of me I didn't know what to order. Then I heard someone say "Brandy" and we followed suit.

The next morning, with a slight hangover, I went to the Purser's office with my letter of introduction from the *Atlanta Constitution.* Immediately, Nammie and I were given the run of the ship. Foremost in my mind was to see the Passenger List to learn what famous people were on board. Before the Bremen landed at Cherbourg I had managed to talk with Anita Loos, whose comedy *Gentlemen Prefer Blondes* had become a national best seller. Also Max Schmeling who had recently won the world's heavy weight boxing title from Jack Sharkey, and the beautiful silent screen star Norma Talmadge, who was obviously having a romantic affair with her travelling companion, the dashing film star Gilbert Roland.

Seeing Paris for the first time was an unbelievable experience. I have probably returned to that beautiful City a hundred times since then, and always with a special glow, but nothing can surpass the thrill of that first visit. We stayed at a charming and most important, inexpensive hotel on the left bank called Hotel du Calais that someone on the ship had recommended.

A couple of days after our arrival I was surprised to receive a telephone call. Who in the world would know how to reach me in Paris? It was from Caroline White, a girl I had known slightly in Atlanta, who had seen my name in the American Express Register. Since we had told our families to send our mail in care of American Express, that had been almost our first stop.

Caroline said she was in Paris with two girl friends, so we made a date to have lunch together the next day. One of Caroline's friends had a car and they were planning to drive through Switzerland and then to the South of France. When they invited us to join them, we accepted immediately. It turned out to be a wonderful adventure and so did the whole European trip.

President of The Student Body at Oglethorpe University

Chapter Two

As I noted earlier, I must have been born with a fascination for fame because upon graduation from Oglethorpe I had a number of business opportunities offered to me in Atlanta but I wasn't interested. Hollywood was a magic name in those days and I was eager to become a part of this extraordinary industry that had only recently introduced sound with films.

It was late September, 1932, and I was making preparations to leave for the Coast when I had a call from a childhood friend, Sidney Sanders. Sidney and I had been in the same class in both Grammar School and High School and we shared many of the same interests.

When I used to park cars at the baseball stadium to make money for trips to New York, Sidney often came and parked cars with me. Then while waiting for the baseball game to be over, to collect our money, we would sit in one of the cars and dream about life in New York and Hollywood.

At the time I entered college, Sidney had gone to New York seeking a career as a writer. I knew he had great talent but as we talked on the phone that day I realized he had been sidetracked and for the past few years had been living a more or less Bohemian life in Greenwich Village.

I told Sidney I was leaving shortly for Hollywood and the next day there was a call from his mother. She said, "Earl, how are you going to Hollywood?" and I answered, "I'm going the cheapest way I can. It's called a jitney service and you travel by car and share the ride with others."

Mrs. Sanders then said, "Earl, you've always been a good influence on my son. I want Sidney to go to California with you, and I'm going to give him the money for the trip."

A few days later, off we went. I've never known such an adventure. It took three or four days just to get to Dallas. From there we drove to El Paso and then on to Phoenix, Arizona. It was slow driving, and at one point we had to change to another group of drivers to get to California. When finally, after five days, we started to go through the desert, Sidney and I really began to get excited. To think, "My God, California is only a hundred miles away." "It's seventy miles away." "It's only fifty miles away." With every passing minute we were building up excitement and thinking it must have been like this for the pioneers who crossed the country in covered wagons when they saw the Pacific Ocean for the first time.

It was a balmy night when we finally reached the outskirts of Los Angeles. There was a gentle breeze and we could see the palm trees swaying and smell the Eucalyptus trees that lined both sides of the road. Eureka! Eureka! At last we were there. The sign said Los Angeles City Limits but suddenly I realized we didn't know where to go. Then I thought the best thing to do was to go to the YMCA. We checked in at the "Y" in downtown Los Angeles and spent the next day exploring the old Spanish section of the City.

We were eager to get to Hollywood, and inquired at the desk the next morning the best way to get there. A young chap at the information desk ahead of us was making the same inquiry. Sidney struck up a conversation with him learning that his name was Lewis Gerard, that he had recently graduated from the University of Indiana and was an aspiring writer. The three of us took a bus into Hollywood. It was almost an hour's trip but we were all eyes and as excited as a five year old on Christmas Eve.

We walked up and down Hollywood Boulevard looking at each person we passed, hoping to spot a movie star, and we must have spent an hour in front of Grauman's Chinese theater looking at the famous signatures and footprints.

The three of us — Sidney, Lew and I — returned the next day and then on the third day we decided to look for an apartment that we could share. On Whitley Avenue, just north of Hollywood Boulevard, we found the perfect one at the Ojai. It was furnished with all utilities included for $45 a month. This meant only $15 each. It had twin beds, so each week we would draw lots to see who would sleep on the sofa in the living room.

Almost immediately, Sidney got a job as a reporter on the *Hollywood Citizen News* and within a very short time he was its drama critic. In this post he received passes to everything. He would come home from work and announce, "Tonight we can have dinner at the Brown Derby or Perino's, and I have tickets for the Jane Cowl play downtown at the Biltmore, or a tryout of a new comedy at Pantages or a screening at Paramount."

I used to say, "But Sidney, we can't do it all in one evening. Why don't you spread it out so that we can go somewhere tomorrow evening, too." But he was so pleased and excited with his newly acquired power of being offered free tickets that he would get them all for the same night. We would end up giving passes to everyone in the apartment building, and then sit home with nothing to do the rest of the week.

Shortly after we arrived in California I wrote a letter to William Randolph Hearst requesting an appointment. A few weeks later there was a telephone call from someone at the *Los Angeles Examiner* saying Mr. Hearst would see me the following Wednesday at 11 A.M. in the executive offices of the Hearst Corporation in downtown Los Angeles.

On the appointed day, I was up at dawn, excited and slightly nervous, thinking of what I was going to say to this powerful man who controlled a publishing empire.

I arrived shortly before the appointed time and was asked by a very pleasant secretary to wait in the reception room. A moment later I was taken in to meet Mr. Hearst's aide de camp, Colonel Joseph Willicomb, who said, "Young man, Mr. Hearst is seeing you today but I want you to know that you're very privileged. He receives hundreds of letters every day from people who want to meet him but he doesn't have the time. You are a very fortunate young man."

I thanked him, and tried to think back to what I had written in my letter that had triggered Mr. Hearst's curiosity and made him agree to this meeting. I recall saying I had been in college with his son, Jack, and that during my freshman year at Oglethorpe, while my parents were spending the Winter in Florida, I had lived on the campus in Phoebe Hearst Hall, named for his mother.

Suddenly the big double oak doors opened and I could see Mr. Hearst sitting behind a huge desk in the adjoining room. Colonel Willicomb took my arm and we walked in together.

I was almost tongue-tied but I managed somehow to smile and thank him for seeing me.

He nodded, and in a very thin voice asked, "Now what is it that you want to do?"

I said I was terribly interested in the motion picture industry and would like to become a part of it."

"Doing what?" he asked, and I said, "I don't know." I then went on to tell about the plays I had written, produced and directed while in college. After a few more questions and answers, Mr. Hearst ended the interview by saying he would try to arrange for me to meet Louis B. Mayer.

I was on Cloud 9, when the following week, Colonel Willicomb called to say the appointment for me to meet Mr. Mayer had been set for Wednesday morning at 11 A.M. in the executive office at MGM.

Louis B. Mayer was the Czar of Hollywood and the following Wednesday as I dressed for the appointment, I carefully chose a most subdued shirt and tie, having read somewhere that Mr. Mayer was most conservative in everything from clothes to horses. I also made sure to get an early start that Wednesday morning because to get from Hollywood to MGM, if you didn't have a car (which I didn't) you would have to take a bus to Washington Boulevard then transfer to a streetcar, and then after an hour and a half on the bus and streetcar you would reach Culver City but you still would have a half-mile walk to MGM. That morning after I reached Culver City and started the long walk to the studio there was a cloudburst. I was soaking wet, drenched from head to toe, when I was ushered into Mr. Mayer's office.

After I told Mr. Mayer of my eagerness to be a part of the film industry, he looked at me with an expression of deep sadness and spoke in a most somber tone. "This is the depth of Depression. It's the worst time we've ever gone through. If I had my own brother's son here I couldn't do anything for him." He then went on painting the darkest picture imaginable.

I was, naturally, devastated but as I thanked him and stood up to go, he said, "Have you ever done any acting?"

"In just a few college plays that I wrote and directed" came my answer. Then he said, I

Chapter Four

In early 1937 I arrived in New York with *April Fool* under my arm. I was anxious to show it to Leland Hayward whom I had heard was one of the leading agents in New York. I checked into a small West Side hotel and hurried over to the Hayward office on Madison Avenue. There I was told that Mr. Hayward was out of town, but to leave the manuscript, and they would be in touch with me on Hayward's return.

Returning to my dreary hotel room with one window that looked out onto a dark court yard, I realized that after the open spaces of California, the small hotel room seemed like a jail cell. I began looking through the want ads for a place to live, when I saw one that caught my eye.

It read: "Sutton Place, Furnished studio room for rent..." I hurried over to the small brownstone building at 41 Sutton Place and was shown the room. It had a high ceiling with a large window, but it had horrible dark green walls and heavy dingy draperies over the large window facing Sutton Place. Discouraged, I left and went looking elsewhere.

That night, back in the dreary hotel room, I started thinking about the Sutton Place studio and what a little white paint would do to brighten it up. Early the next morning I returned to 41 Sutton Place, and asked the elderly French lady who had shown me the room originally, if she would permit me to paint the studio.

"Oh, yes, Monsieur. You are free to do anything you wish with the studio." With that assurance, I bought five gallons of white paint, borrowed a step ladder and started painting away. About one o'clock there was a knock on the door, and in came the French lady carrying a tray of the most delicious French food. She smiled at the young boy at the top of the ladder, saying "Monsieur, you are working too hard. You must take a moment to rest and have some nourishment."

My wonderful Madame's real name was Marie Louise Marilott (Charbonier). She was born in 1887 in Grenoble, a small factory town in the southeast section of France. Her family was very poor.

Marie Louise was a very young girl and at the age of 15 fell in love with the son of the factory owner, Henri Charbonier who was 29. When their romantic affair became a village scandal, he headed for America and she followed six months later.

Marie Louise was a hard worker and at one time owned five or six lingerie shops in New York. They were never legally married, but happily lived together until he died in 1927. The brownstone house at 41 Sutton Place was owned by the city of New York and leased to Madame Charbonier for less than $60 a month.

Besides my studio, Madame rented two other rooms on the second floor to an Irish spinster named, Miss O'Brian, and a third floor connecting room to a French Chef who had

Marie Louis Marilott (My wonderful Madame)

recently worked for J.P. Morgan and later for his daughter, Anne Morgan; whose townhouse on Sutton Place was only a stone's throw away. Since my studio apartment adjoined Madame's three room apartment in the rear, she often invited me to come for breakfast. "Stay in your robe and come have breakfast with me she would say." I have some very good croissants this morning, Monsieur."

Madame became a major figure in my life. She adopted me and I her. Years later I was to be her witness when she became a U.S. citizen. And later, I gave her a small job so that she would eventually be entitled to Social Security.

When I met Leland Hayward, he greeted me by saying, "After reading your play *April Fool,* I expected to see an elderly man hobble in my office with a cane; your detailed description of Broadway in the early part of this century is so well drawn."

Hayward then went on to say that Peggy Fears was in New York looking for new property to turn into a musical; her last production *Music in the Air* was so successful. Hayward thought she might like to produce my play which was about a young woman's life in the theatre and was intended as a musical. He was right. Fears optioned the play for $75 a month and planned to have Jerome Kern write the score as soon as he was available.

I lived on the thrill of this break — and the meager $75 a month for weeks — until Peggy Fears decided that she didn't want Jerome Kern to compose the score; she wanted Cole Porter. I was even more excited. I wrote a second play, *Aries Is Rising* which was produced at the John Golden Theatre with Constance Collier, but lasted just seven performances before it closed. I waited for *April Fool* to come together. And waited and waited and waited.

When I was in Hollywood I found it was the long wait between pictures that was demoralizing and I found Bridge to be the solution to my problem. So I was delighted when Alice Leoni, a screenwriter, invited me to a Bridge game every weekend at her New York apartment. It would begin with lunch on Saturday and end early Sunday morning.

At one of these sessions I ran into a chap who was in the same predicament as I was. He had written a hot line about Cuba and was seeking a publisher. His name was Ted Strong. He had recently spent some time in Cuba. Our mutual friend, Daniel Blum, had taken a small boathouse on Fire Island for the summer. He invited Ted and me for a long Holiday weekend. At the last minute his plans changed. He was going to California for the summer and offered the boathouse to Ted and me. We decided to collaborate on a novel about a southern girl who uncovered a murder while visiting a friend on the island of Nantucket, where Ted was born. Since it was Ted's birthplace, his background information would be accurate.

It was quite a summer and ended with a bang! The famous 1938 hurricane that hit Long Island in early September swept to sea our manuscript along with the boathouse and our personal belongings. We were lucky not to have been swept away ourselves. We had gone into town for two days before the hurricane hit. Just by chance we were invited to second night seats at the new Broadway musical called *Jubilee*. Quite a few messages were waiting for me at Madames. I telephoned Madame twice a week during the summer hoping for messages. Waiting for me was one that caught my eye. It was from Mildred Seydel, a newspaper woman from Atlanta. She was staying at the Warwick Hotel and when I called her, she invited Ted and me to dinner at El Morroco. When we met she said she was on assignment to write profiles of several celebrities, but was having the damndest time trying to track them down. She particularly needed to find Robert Montgomery and Ginger Rogers.

Since I knew both personalities quite well, I took a small black leather book from my suit jacket, thumbed through it, and produced the phone numbers and addresses the reporter so badly needed. She was delighted and said, "You are a regular Information Bureau, Earl."

This is when I conceived the idea for Celebrity Service, and within a couple of months, and a loan of just $300 from my Godmother, Lillian Terry, Celebrity Service was official with a small office on East 54 Street, just near El Morocco.

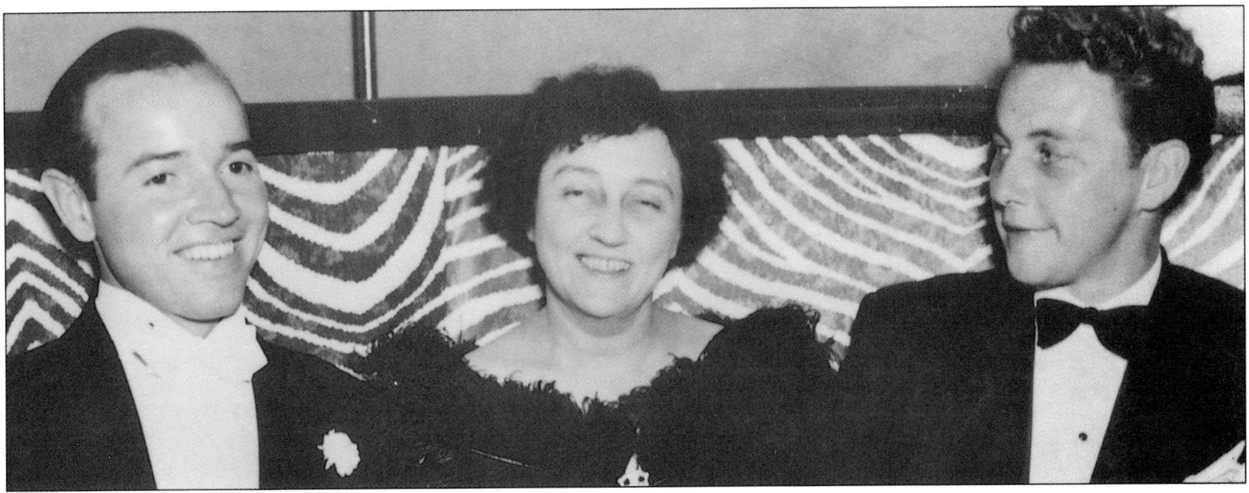

THE DAY CELEBRITY SERVICE WAS BORN

Atlanta newspaper woman, Mildred Seydell, was in New York doing a feature story on celebrities. She was having a difficult time and asked me how she could reach Ginger Rogers. I looked in my black book and gave the information to her. She also asked for Robert Montgomery and when I provided it, she said, "You are a regular Information Bureau, Earl." She took Ted and me to El Morocco to celebrate!

*Frances Van (right) came to me as a teenager fresh out of high school.
Today, she is a grandmother and still works for Celebrity Service.*

Chapter Five

The whole operation of Celebrity Service began on a shoestring. After I had borrowed $300 from my Godmother, I was walking along East 54th Street near El Morocco and saw a studio for rent in a brownstone. It was a big room downstairs on the street floor and a small private stairway leading upstairs to a little apartment. I thought it would be ideal for Celebrity Service downstairs and I could live upstairs and only have to pay one light bill and one telephone bill each month.

I signed the lease and put a sign outside on the mailbox. The first day the bell rang I jumped up with great excitement and went to the door. There was a very attractive lady standing there, but I could tell something was troubling her.

"I just tore up your sign," she said.

"I beg your pardon," I said. I was flabbergasted.

"I just saw that sign – 'CELEBRITY SERVICE.' What are you running, a call house? I tore it up," she replied.

It turned out that she lived in the building and was the wife of William L. White, who later wrote *Journey for Margaret.* He was the son of William Allen White of the Kansas paper. We all became very good friends. In fact, for the first few months of Celebrity Service, when we couldn't even afford to buy a *Who's Who,* if someone would call for a person we didn't have, I'd run upstairs and borrow the White's book.

At the very beginning, it was not exactly clear how Celebrity Service would operate. All we had was a name and my Little Black Book. With no capital whatsoever and no formula to follow, we moved cautiously. I thought we needed an established firm to present Celebrity Service. I happened to know the Vice-President of Promotions at Western Union, but he was away, so I was seeking support in terms of Postal Telegraph. When I spoke with the Public Relations head at Postal Telegraph, he was most enthusiastic and said, "Get yourself organized and we'll make Celebrity Service available to our branch offices" (approximately 20 offices in Manhattan). Once we got the format set, including *The Daily Bulletin* which announced the arrival of celebrities and listed their agents or affiliations, and a massive file for information by telephone, we realized this was not a service for the general public, but rather a valuable source for the Communications industry.

CBS was the very first subscriber to Celebrity Service. They had seen a story about the unique business in one of the columns and called me for an appointment. I went to the interview thinking perhaps they wanted me to go on a radio show and describe my unusual business. When they explained they had twenty-seven radio programs a week requiring guest stars and they wished to subscribe and asked for the monthly fee, I was taken by surprise. We hadn't even decided yet on the amount to charge our clients. So I said, "May I write to you giving all the details?" Then I ran back to the office and debated with Ted what we should charge. We finally decided on ten dollars a month as CBS became our very first subscriber. (Today, Celebrity Service has dozens of subscribers with each paying approximately $300 per month).

After CBS came aboard, it wasn't difficult to get NBC and ABC to sign up. Soon we had Paramount Pictures and Bergdorf Goodman... *Newsweek* and *Vogue*... and BBD&O and Young & Rubicam. Newspapers, advertising agencies, casting agents, the State Department and even the FBI followed shortly thereafter. As each new company subscribed, I was aware that it obviously could prove advantagous to other companies in the same field, so we personally would go after them and point out the advantages of a subscription to Celebrity Service. After several months, we could afford a much-needed secretary. We were working till almost midnight every night to make sure that *The Daily Bulletin* was hand delivered to each subscriber every weekday morning. It was a very exciting time.

With Godmother Lillian Terry who gave me a $300 loan to start Celebrity Service...

Chapter Six:

The World's Fair of 1940 was the most wonderful opportunity to come our way. We'd gotten a bit of publicity and were just managing to keep our heads above water when the bonanza of all time happened. Harvey Gibson, the President of Manufacturers Trust Company, was made director of the 1940 Fair. He had read about Celebrity Service and called me. We met on a snowy day in March and drove to the fairground. Gibson said how much he wanted celebrities at the Fair, but couldn't afford to pay them their huge fees. He said, "I'll give you $150.00 a week and put a car and driver at your disposal, and you can invite any celebrity you want to be guest of the World's Fair."

Well, that was fabulous for us. We arranged a Helen Hayes Day, Amos and Andy Day, Gertrude Lawrence Day, Noel Coward Day, etc. When I heard Noel was coming over to New York, I sent him a cable saying, "We'd like to have Noel Coward Day at the World's Fair." He accepted graciously and asked if he could bring Constance Collier. I was delighted, particularly because I had grown so fond of her during the short run of my play, *Aries Is Rising* in which she starred. For his day, I arranged for every exhibit at the Fair to play Noel's music from 6 PM to midnight.

At World's Fair with Lois January

I arrived with Noel at the Fair at four minutes to 6 o'clock and I asked the driver to wait outside the gate for a few minutes (knowing the music was set to begin). As we waited in the car, Noel assumed I had a huge crowd assembled to greet him and when we finally drove through the gates he kidded me, "Where are my fans?" However, when he actually heard his music coming over the loudspeakers, he became more than delighted and thought that was terrific.

Tallulah Bankhead

I was with Tallulah Bankhead having dinner at the French Pavillion on her day at the Fair. It was when we received the horrible news that France had fallen. Tallulah vowed that day she wouldn't drink another drop of alcohol until France was back on its feet again. I'm not sure she kept at this vow.

Tallulah became a great friend. During the War, she was on the road in a show when she called me one afternoon. "Earl," she began, "I'm coming into town at the end of the week and I need a two bedroom apartment suite in a hotel." "But my God, Tallulah," I protested, "There's a war on. There's a great shortage."

She'd have none of that. "You call yourself Celebrity Service? Well, I'm a celebrity and I want some service." And she got it.

One evening I was having dinner with my father who was in New York on a visit from Atlanta. Since my mother had passed away, my father who was lonely came to see me quite frequently. On that particular night we were in the Cub Room of the Stork Club and Tallulah was sitting at a table nearby. She beckoned me over and asked, "Who is the distinguished man with you?"

When I told her it was my father, she said, "Bring him over."

Father was very pleased to meet Tallulah and they talked about many things and finally got on the subject of horses and racing; one of my father's favorite subjects. The evening ended by father inviting Tallulah to accompany him to the Belmont stakes the next day. She accepted at once, then turned to me and whispered, "Darling, I may be your stepmother yet."

I waved to the two of them as they drove off to Belmont the next morning. Tallulah looking particularly stunning in a tailored wool jacket and matching slacks. When they arrived at the race track, and started to enter the special reserved box section, they were halted by a uniformed guard who stated rather bluntly, "Ladies are not permitted in this section wearing slacks." With that father put out his arm and said, "Move away, son, This is Miss Tallulah Bankhead, the distinguished actress and her father happens to be the Speaker of the House." And in they walked. Tallulah used to love to tell that story.

Many opportunities came my way as a result of the Summer of 1940. It was at the World's Fair that I first met Sonja Henie, the young little blonde Norwegian who had won her first Olympic ice skating championship at the age of 15 and a total of ten world championships, plus three Olympic firsts in figure skating. Her peaches and cream freshness made her a top film star in the thirties. After two failed marriages (to Yankee owner, Dan Topping and yachtsman, Winthrop Gardiner, Jr.) she married "Oslo's Onassis" Niels Onstad in 1956. Years later, Sonja and her husband contacted me to organize the $8 million Art Center in Oslo. This was one of my first international events. I was able to arrange for Angier Biddle Duke, Perle Mesta, Dame Margot Fonteyn and Aga Khan. My greatest coup was to have the King of Norway attend.

Sonja Henie and her husband, shipowner Niels Onstad, beside Pablo Picasso's "Two Fish in the Kitchen;" one of 116 paintings at the art center in Oslo, Norway where I arranged the opening festivities.

To
my dearest Earl,
a wonderful friend,
With much love,
Caline
1953

Chapter Seven

In 1950, I was surprised one morning when I received a formal letter from Ted Strong, my partner over this past decade, saying that he wanted to sell his interest in Celebrity Service. He said that he had thought about it a long time and consulted our lawyer to draw up the necessary agreement. Ted said, now that the business was stable, he could travel without being tied down to a desk. He thought $50,000 would be fair and he hoped I could buy him out. This was a shock, but a happy one for although Ted had contributed and worked hard, he was a conservative New-Englander and held me back from potential promotion and publicity.

To raise enough money to pay Ted, I sold a house on Long Island and cashed in some stocks that I had accumulated through the years from my Aunt's Christmas presents. I leaped at the chance to have complete control and the opportunity to develop any new ideas for promoting the business. My first step on my own was moving the office from the Brownstone on 54th Street, next to El Morocco, to 631 Fifth Avenue.

Up to now, we had just a representative in Hollywood, so I made plans to open a regular office with a Daily West Coast Bulletin and Telephone Service. I flew out to California to organize this branch office and one of the first things I did was visit the little church across from MGM. During the short time I was under contract to MGM as an actor, I used to stop by that little church every day and ask God to please let me be a success. This time I wanted to thank HIM for not answering my original prayer; this taught me a lesson. In my daily prayers I never ask God for anything specific, but always ask HIM to continue to guide me and give me HIS Blessings.

While I was in California seeking old friends and making new ones, I used to go to parties every Sunday night at the home of Cobina Wright who lived in Beverly Hills, just above "Pickfair." Cobina was a legendary person in the society world of New York in the 1920's. As a matter of fact, in her book *I Never Grew Up* she tells about her romance with General Pershing just after World War I. Cobina married William Wright and became a big hostess on Long Island. Then in 1929, everything crashed. Wright lost all his money and Cobina lost him. She started to sing in Supper Clubs in New York before she moved out to Los Angeles. It was her daughter, Cobina Wright Jr., who was the famous debutante who almost married Prince Philip before he married Elizabeth.

I met Marion Davies through Cobina Wright. Mr. Hearst had given Cobina a daily society column on the Los Angeles *Examiner,* thus giving her a lot of power, which she enjoyed. At one of her famous parties, Marion Davies was there; this was when Mr. Hearst was still alive but did not accompany her on account of being ill.

Marion was drinking champagne and was very gay and lovely. She was a very exuberant person and seemed to take a fancy to me. She kept going up to Cobina and saying, "You know, I like Earl. I think I'm going to marry him."

Cobina, laughing, told Marion to stand in line. But, all evening long, Marion kept saying, "Cobina, I think I really want to marry Earl." Finally, Cobina said, "Alright, let's get down to the wedding right now."

She appointed Gene Tierney the maid of honor and Robert Stack the best man. She positioned Marion and me and went to the piano and played the Wedding March. When she played "Here Comes The Bride" Marion marched in and we had a mock wedding.

Bright and early the next morning Marion was on the phone to Cobina. "Where's my husband?" she asked.

"I locked him up in the ice box," Cobina answered.

Another friendship that has meant so much to me that began with Cobina Wright is my Parisian friend, Roger Dann. He had a most interesting career. His first visit to Hollywood began where Paramount assigned him as a replacement for Maurice Chevalier. After a couple of Broadway plays, Roger's biggest success came in London where he played the leading male role in SOUND OF MUSIC for over two years.

I also met Virginia Warren (daughter of Chief Justice & Mrs. Earl Warren) at one of Cobina's parties. When Virginia came to New York with her mother, Perle Mesta was also in town and I decided to give a small dinner for all of them. A highpoint of the evening was Mrs. Warren's description of her first White House dinner. Mrs. Warren had telephoned the hotel operator for a limousine to drive her and her husband to the White House. When the time came, they went down to the lobby to find a big 24-seat limousine waiting for them. She laughed as she described their ride and embarrassment when the President greeted them at the door.

The 1950's was an exciting and very active decade for me. Bebe Daniels was visiting New York when I met her. This acclaimed silent screen star who moved into sound and starred in such classics as *42nd Street* and *Flying Down To Rio* was married to Ben Lyon; the couple had a very popular radio show in London and they endeared themselves to all English when they stayed in London right through the War. People loved them for it.

Bebe told me that I must open a London Bureau of Celebrity Service. She said, "They desperately need you." I replied, "Find me someone to run it and I'll do the rest..." She came to me two weeks later and said she had the perfect person for the job. Her name was Jeannie Hoskins, the wife of Percy Hoskins - the famed crime reporter. My attorney at the time, Howard Reinhammel, also represented Richard Rodgers and Oscar Hammerstein, was on his way to London for *South Pacific*. I asked him if he would meet Miss Hoskins and tell me if he

with Virginia Warren in N.Y.C.

thought she could run the office. He returned with a strong "Yes" and said, "She is perfect for you, Earl."

I arranged during the Spring of 1952, to spend a month in London, meeting contacts and building the foundation for Celebrity Service's first overseas outfit. We had a big opening splash with all the London Press attending. With the London office off to a good start, I decided to tackle Paris.

Elsa Schiaparelli and Francoise de Langlaid who was the editor of French VOGUE, took me in hand and saw to it that I met everyone. Within a short period of time, I was being invited to luncheons, country-for-the-weekends, and all the top social functions. When I first arrived in Paris, I stayed at the Hotel Crillon which was facing the Place de Concorde and one of the top hotels in France. I had been told by Amy Friend that the old maid rooms in the attic of the Crillon had recently been turned into bachelor quarters; the ideal living quarters to fit into my budget. The surprise of all time came when the week after my arrival, I had a call from Max Bluet of the George V Hotel inviting me to lunch. I was pleased for I had heard his hotel was very popular with Americans. During lunch, I was overwhelmed when Mr. Bluet said, "I'm so happy you're in town to open Celebrity Service. I have read a lot about your New York office and we need that type of information in Paris." He said, "I'd like to extend an invitation for you to be our guest during your stay." I didn't quite understand this invitation, so he repeated that he wanted me to be a guest at his hotel. It seemed all too good to be true, but I accepted the invitation, and I must say that through the years it paid off for him. I sent everyone to his hotel including, Joan Crawford and Alfred Steele, Cary Grant, Dolores and Bob Hope, Patrice Munsel and Bob Schuler, Dorothy and Alfred Strelsin, and all the Gabors: Eva, Zsa Zsa, Magda and Mama.

The opening of the Celebrity Office in London, 1952.
Pictured here with Jeannie Hoskins, Julie Wilson and Baron Polan.

to Earl Blackwell
I give you the prize
for the most charming
man of the festival.
Cannes le 30 Avril 53

Leslie Caron

Chapter Eight

I met Olivia De Havilland for the first time in 1953 at a luncheon in New York given by the Consulate General of France. We both had been invited to attend the Cannes Film Festival as guests of the French government and the luncheon was just prior to take off that afternoon for Cannes. At the luncheon, I was seated next to Olivia and her first words to me were, "I'm so glad to meet the man I am sleeping with tonight." There was a twinkle in her eye and a devilish smile on her face. She meant of course that we would be sitting next to one another aboard the TWA evening flight to Paris. I learned later at the airport that she was also travelling with her young six year old son, Benjamin, and his nurse, who sat in the two seats in front of us.

In those days the trip by air to Europe took twelve hours with a brief stop in New Foundland. I remember after dinner on board, Olivia excused herself for a moment, and then returned in a negligee and house coat. When we arrived in Paris the next morning, she had changed back into a stunning suit.

We were met at Orly by a good friend of mine, Pierre Galante of PARIS MATCH. Pierre had been very helpful to me the preceding year in obtaining my Carte de Commerce in order to open my Paris bureau. As we stepped off the plane I introduced Pierre to Olivia; a year later, they were married.

We stayed overnight in Paris and left the following day for Nice, where limousines were waiting to drive us to Cannes. Having spent three or four weeks in the South of France the previous summer, as a house guest of Jacques Sarlie and Rosita Winston, I knew that part of France very well. I asked the driver if we could take the scenic route along the shore line instead of the express way through the mountains. It was a joy to see that part of the world again.

The Carlton Hotel in Cannes was a beehive of activity. There were more than a dozen photographers and an equal amount of journalists trying to interview the film stars. The first person to grab my arm and say "hello" was Zsa Zsa Gabor who was with George Sanders, her husband at that time. Then I noticed Kirk Douglas talking with Anne Baxter and Errol Flynn trying to get past three photographers at the front entrance. As I waited in line to register and be assigned a room, a most attractive French girl introduced herself and welcomed me to the Festival. Her name was Anne Buydens. She later became Mrs. Kirk Douglas and they recently celebrated their 35th Anniversary. Anne handed me a program outlining the events of the three-day Festival. I was pleased to see that I was listed in the Program as escort to Leslie Caron. I had written to Leslie telling her I was coming and she, no doubt, arranged it to be in the Program, also giving the time and place of the special luncheons, dinners and screenings that I would attend.

Cannes
Film Festival

Top Right:
with Philip Reed

Above:
with Errol Flynn
(Photo: Pierre Mancient)

Left: *Pictured in front of the
Carlton Hotel (Cannes) are
Jacques Fath, Patricia (a French Model),
Rock Hudson and Je Royce Landis*
(Photo: Ed Quinn)

Right: *One day in Cannes I picked up
a few pals to go sightseeing.
Among them, Anne Baxter and
French Film star, Arletty.*

— ⬦ —

I thought how fortunate I was to be meeting not only film stars from all over the globe but top executives of the industry, who would be of great assistance to me, now that I was starting to open offices of Celebrity Service in Italy, France and England.

On my visit to Paris in 1985, twenty-two years later, I telephoned Olivia De Havilland and asked her to lunch with me at the Crillon. It was a beautiful day; we lunched in the garden of the Crillon, with all eyes turned on our table.

It had been a number of years since we had seen one another and I was happy to note that the serene beauty of Olivia's face was more evident now that it was framed with hair streaked with grey. The eyes still had the merry twinkle and we had fun recalling the time we were

In Paris with Olivia De Havilland and Maurice Chevalier

Olivia De Havilland (at 25th Anniversary of "Gone With The Wind")

invited to Atlanta by Mary Lou and Sonny Whitney for the second world premiere of *"Gone With The Wind"*...During the scene in the film where Scarlett is assisting Melanie with the birth of her baby, Olivia turned to me in the theater and said, "Last year in Paris, a big six foot seven soldier came up to me and said, 'Miss De Havilland, I'm the baby boy you once held in your arms.' "

In 1954 I was invited again to the CANNES & VENICE Film Festivals and this time I decided to give a party in Venice in early September. I had a small budget so I wrote to Venice's head of special events and he cabled that they were delighted to assist me in any way possible.

At the beginning of that Summer I went to Venice and was treated like a royal prince. I was wined and dined and taken to several different palaces the officials thought I might like for my party. We decided on the Palazzo Vendere Clergi, which is where Wagner died. It was magnificent, with an entrance on the Grand Canal. Once I knew where the party was to be held, I telephoned my secretary, Miss Phoenix, in New York and the invitations were prepared and mailed. I'd left my list already arranged with Miss Phoenix so all she had to do was fill in the date and place. Then, I spent the interim in the South of France.

I returned to Venice two weeks before the party only to discover the press had gone wild. They heard that the invitations read: "The Celebrity Party" and that the guests were asked to come dressed as any celebrity of this century. Katharine Hepburn was in Italy filming *Summertime*. The local press ran a picture of her alongside one of Amelia Earhart, saying that was who Hepburn planned to dress as. Marlene Dietrich, they wrote, planned on coming as Mistinguette. Awaiting my arrival were 275 requests from the foreign press to cover the party! I was baffled. The party had been blown way out of proportion.

Fortunately, the head of the American Film Institute cornered me shortly after my arrival and asked if they couldn't join forces with me, as they had a large budget for entertaining and my party sounded so exciting. I was delighted and felt as if I had been saved from a burning volcano. All seemed serene until, the night before the party when I was called out to the Lido for a meeting to go over last minute details with the various contingencies. When I arrived, however, I was told bad news. At the last minute the use of the Palace was being revoked. I was dumbfounded.

I pleaded with the officials: "What do you mean? People are just arriving from London, New York, California..." All I was told was that the Mayor of Venice had decided to withdraw the palace. I would soon find out it was all Elsa Maxwell's doing. She'd been a good friend until that point, but suddenly because of all the publicity, I had become an upstart.

Elsa Maxwell liked to say she was born in a theatre box in Keokuk, Iowa during a performance of Mignon. One of Elsa's most amusing traits was that she often made fun of herself. She liked to play the piano and sing. People enjoyed that and she was fun to be with until perhaps her ego became too inflated.

When I first came to New York, I found Elsa to be very friendly. She always made overtures to me when I walked into the Colony or the Stork Club and she was there. "Come right over and talk to me," she would insist.

I was often invited to play cards on Sunday nights at her apartment in the Waldorf and she always included me in her large dinner dances in Paris. We were good friends until I decided to give the party in Paris. Elsa was quoted as saying, "How dare another American give a party here." She must have thought that giving parties in Venice was her perogative only. Elsa told the Mayor that having my party at the Palazzo was an awful risk. "Just too many people," she caimed, "It might damage your beautiful Palace."

I was told at the same meeting that the American Film Institute had also decided to withdraw their financial support. Someone convinced them, and so they were now claiming, that I'd received all the publicity and they'd gotten none.

I was speechless. At that point, a man sitting in the back of the room called out, "That's a lie and I'm going to print it." He was the head of the Associated Press in Italy and I could bless him forever. He stood up and said: "I've seen all the press announcements about this party." He asserted, "and your name and Earl Blackwell's has always been equally associated."

They finally agreed not to withdraw their financial support. They did withdraw their name, however.

I was devastated when I walked outside; I wasn't prepared for the three dozen reporters wanting to know if there was going to be a Celebrity Party and where it would be held. I thought quickly and told them to come meet me at my hotel at midnight and I'd tell them the new location. They were like a pack of animals that needed feeding.

Elsa Maxwell

It was nearly seven o'clock when I returned to Venice and began to seek a new location. I went first to the Bauer Gunwald on the Grand Canal. The manager greeted me warmly and said, "Oh, Mr. Blackwell, we would like nothing better than having the great celebrity party at our hotel, but since it will start at ten o'clock it would disturb some of our guests. By this time, everyone in Venice knew about the party. It was the talk of the aristocrats as well as the workmen. I went from one place to another until I arrived at the Cafe Martini, which had an entrance on a Canal. This ingredient was important, I felt. The owner was home sick and so I went to his house. He said he had read so much about the Celebrity party and would be happy to have it but it meant closing his cafe for both lunch and dinner the next day. After much persuasion he agreed and after signing a contract (I was taking no chances), I returned to the hotel shortly after midnight and told the waiting press that the party would be at the Martini that evening.

Despite Elsa Maxwell's attempts to sabotage the party, it turned out to be a great success. Arturo Lopez, a South American social King who owned the yacht where Elsa was staying, told me that he had never been to a better party and Elsa had tried every trick in the book to have him leave earlier to miss this extraordinary evening.

For many years following this encounter with Elsa, when attending a large party in New York, I would quickly scan the room to see if I saw Elsa or heard her voice. Then, I would walk to the opposite side of the room. This evasive plan didn't work the night of Edith Baker's party for the Duke and Duchess of Windsor. I managed to avoid Elsa during the cocktail hour, but when I walked into the dining room and saw that I was sitting next to Elsa, it was too late to ask the hostess to change. It was awkward for a brief moment, then we both pretended that nothing had ever happened between us. When dinner was over and we were going into the drawing room, I offered Elsa my arm. She was, by that time, already crippled with age.

Some friends who knew about our troubles were surprised by the warmth we shared that evening and I'm so glad we had a chance to make up.

You know, when Elsa was just a girl in San Francisco she was told she was "too poor" to rate an invitation to the wedding of a Vanderbilt. She had to watch from the street and Elsa was beside herself. "I made up my mind there and then" she vowed, "that some day I would give great parties all over the world and that no one would give more parties with less Vanderbilts than I would." And she did.

Chapter Nine

In the mid-fifties, Noel was in New York and called me saying he had heard I was about to leave for Europe and could he rent my apartment during my absence. In those days I was living in a small three-room apartment at Regency House on West 54th Street, just off Fifth Avenue. I was delighted as I planned to be away two or three months opening offices in London, Paris and Rome.

The next day Noel stopped by to finalize the arrangements when he noticed a small baby grand piano I had bought second hand to use for parties. Noel started to play but it was horribly out of tune. He said he definitely wanted the apartment because he would be in New York all summer working on a new play but would I mind if he rented a small piano. I told him of course I didn't mind.

That evening I started to think: Noel Coward living in my apartment and composing a new score. I really should have a proper piano. I called Noel and asked him to please meet me at Steinway the next morning to select a new grand piano. He did, and it was on that piano he wrote the score to *Sail Away,* and it has a prominent place in my ballroom today. It was also on this piano that young Emanuel Ax practiced when he immigrated to this country with his father and mother and lived with me, but that's another story which I will speak of later.

We all know how witty Noel Coward was, but he was also a man of deep feelings and loyalty. I remember in 1940 Laurence Olivier and Vivien Leigh were in New York doing *Romeo and Juliet* at the Ziegfeld Theater. One evening Noel invited me to join them for supper after the performance. Great Britain was already at war and at dinner no one talked about anything else. Noel kept trying to remind Larry of his obligation to return to England and join the War Effort. Olivier was enjoying a great success on Broadway and he and Vivien were deeply in love and happy at that point; he was reluctant to give it all up. Noel finally persuaded him and a few weeks later Larry was back home and in service. His contribution was outstanding and of course Larry subsequently became Lord Olivier.

When Noel was knighted and I heard he was due to arrive in New York, I took over Raffles on a Sunday night and gave a memorable party in his honor. It was also his seventieth birthday. Peggy Wood sang "I'll See You Again," which she had introduced in the London Company of *Bitter Sweet,* and Kay Thompson and Bobby Short played double pianos. Everyone came: Cary Grant, Myrna Loy, Ethel Merman, Gloria Vanderbilt, Douglas Fairbanks, Jr., Joan Fontaine, Diana Vreeland, Paul Newman, Warren Beatty, Tammy Grimes, Merle Oberon, Anita Loos, Ann Woodward and Fred Astaire, to name a few.

If any British subject ever deserved to be knighted, Noel certainly did. He was a composer, author, playwright, actor, singer, director, and night club entertainer. A brilliant man of the theater, although for years the critics said that his vogue could not possibly last.

with Noel Coward and Cary Grant

Top left:
Noel Coward and Hermione Gingold

Below:
Peggy Wood

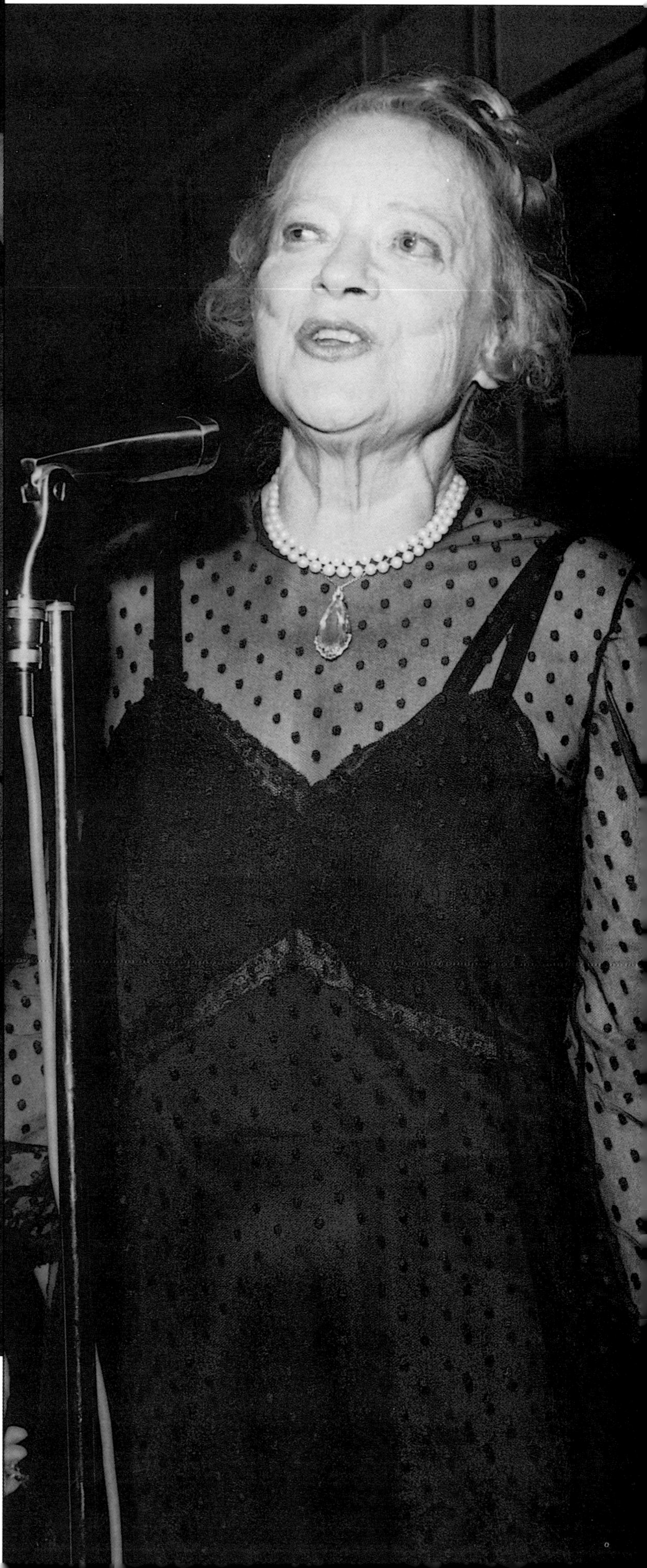

Above:
Myrna Loy congratulates Noel Coward at Knighthood party

Left: *Anne Slater and Cary Grant*

Above:
*At RAFFLES Party
for NOEL COWARD'S "Knighthood"
Earl Wilson, Elaine Stritch and Tammy Grimes*

Far left:
Bobby Short & Kay Thompson

Left: Jule Styne

— 55 —

His friends were overjoyed that Noel had finally been knighted and my party was a great success. That morning Mary Lee Fairbanks had called to tell me that she and Douglas had arrived only that morning from Bali to find my invitation. She then telephoned Noel to regret, explaining, "I don't think we will be able to come, Noel. We've just flown here from around the world. My hair has not been washed for a week and I look a mess."

Coward answered, "Don't be silly. Who do you think will be looking at you? They will be looking at me."

Noel Coward & Douglas Fairbanks, Jr.

Gloria Swanson

Chapter Ten

I'd known Gloria Swanson from the time I was a teenager, on my first visit to New York where I saw her making a silent film at the old Astoria Studio. Then later in Hollywood we became good friends. In 1962, the Italian Line asked me to help them publicize their luxury liner, the LEONARDO da VINCI.

As Celebrity Service grew and became international, so did our Special Events department. I found myself organizing a resort in Mexico for Antenor Patino, The Love Party in Paris for Mary Wells Lawrence, A Red & White Party at Eden Roc and so on…

One of the most interesting and challenging projects was this Mediterranean cruise. In early December, the Italian Line called me down to their office explaining they had the flagship of the Mediterranean, the LEONARDO da VINCI, sailing on a six-week cruise in early February. They explained that they had advertised the cruise without any success and wanted to know if I could assist them. I suggested they assign me twelve staterooms and invite celebrities as my guests. These celebrities would be under no obligation to perform, just to enjoy the cruise.

The Italian Line, of course, could publicize the fact that Paul Newman, Joanne Woodward, Gloria Swanson, Joan Fontaine, Charles Addams, Ruth Ford and Zachary Scott would be travelling. The cruise sold out within a few weeks.

Gloria Swanson had an entire stateroom just for her clothes. The press clamored for interviews at every port. Gloria was 100% a star. Still, she was always polite when an elderly person entered the room, she'd stand up. Gloria criticized Joanne Woodward for failing to follow her example on the trip.

At one luncheon while we were docked at Capri, our waitress, a middle age Cockney woman, told us her name was Gloria. When she went into the kitchen, Gloria Swanson turned to me and said, quite matter-of-factly, "That is not her real name."

"Why in the world do you say that?" I asked.

"Because she must be my age and no one had the name Gloria until I was famous," she said.

I thought that was a bit unlikely until I happened to go into the kitchen to change an order. While speaking to our waitress I mentioned that the lady in dark glasses at my table was Gloria Swanson. She dropped the tray she was holding and said, "My God, she's been my screen idol all my life. When she cut her hair for *Manhandled* I cut mine. I even changed my name to Gloria. My real name is Agnes."

Gloria was extremely intelligent. By strict diet she was able to cure herself of cancer and she went on a national campaign against pesticides, even making an appearance in Washington before Congress. She was very direct and honest in everything she did. She also

*Gloria Swanson & Carol Channing (pictured here with Tallulah Bankhead) were "cheap" dinner guests.
Always health conscious, Gloria & Carol brought their own food to any dinner party they attended.*

At a party for "Redhead" star Gwen Verdon (2nd from right): Ginger, Gloria & Ethel (l-r) were among those sharing in the celebration.

saved everything, including letters and contracts going back to the very beginning of her career. They are now in the archives of the University of Texas in Austin. An interesting letter on file is from a twelve year old boy scout named John F. Kennedy, thanking her for a Christmas gift.

In her autobiography, *Swanson on Swanson* published in 1980, three years before her death, she inscribed my book saying, "To Earl, my dear, dear friend of many, many years from another one who loves him deeply, Gloria."

She was a wonderful friend and we shared many happy times together. I recall being with her in New York at the time of the 1951 Academy Awards. She was appearing on Broadway in a play, so could not be in Hollywood for the ceremony. However, there was no doubt in anyone's mind that Gloria would certainly win the Oscar for her outstanding performance in *Sunset Boulevard.* When the winner was announced that evening, and Judy Holliday was the winner, Gloria smiled, and like the thoroughbred she was, took the defeat graciously.

Gloria fell madly in love with Brian Degas towards the end of her life. It didn't work out very well, to say the least. He took some of the love letters Micky Neilan had written to her, but the children were able to get them back. In a way it was *Sunset Boulevard* played all over again, with Gloria very much in love with a younger man.

Remembering the LEONARDO da VINCI cruise, when I was originally approached by the Italian Line, I stipulated in my contract that besides inviting twelve celebrities to join the cruise, I wanted to take my loyal secretary, Vine Phoenix. It was agreed, and I'll never forget returning to the office and saying to Miss Phoenix "One of your Christmas presents this year will be a six weeks Mediterranean Cruise."

At the time, I was quite sincere and never dreamed of the work in store for both of us. At every port we were entertained by heads of State: the King of Morocco, or some dignatery equally well known. This meant a constant flow of cable and long distance calls, making all arrangements for the celebrity group, before landing at each port, and then afterwards all the thank you notes.

Miss Phoenix, as a young girl, used to be an expert horseback rider. So before leaving New York she said, "I'm taking along my riding clothes, so that when we visit Egypt I can climb on top of a camel and have my picture taken to send my mother." We docked in Alexandria, Egypt and drove by motor to Cairo. This was my second visit to Egypt. The first time had been several years earlier when I had been invited by Conrad Hilton to fly there for the official opening of his Nile Hilton Hotel. It was nice to return to the same hotel after a few years and see how popular it had become. On our first evening in Cairo our party was entertained on the roof of the Hilton by the General Manager. It was the night we heard the exciting news that for the first time a young American had orbited the earth in a space capsule. I recall shouts of joy from everyone as we toasted the new American hero, John Glenn.

Everyone was anxious to see the pyramids, so we made plans to meet in the lobby of the hotel at 9:30 AM the next morning. Our host, the General Manager, said he would arrange cars for us and in passing he said, "Mr. Blackwell, you might tell the members of your party that the Egyptians frown on ladies in slacks." I thanked him, and then told Miss Phoenix to pass the word on to the other ladies in the party.

Miss Phoenix, who is always so affable and agreeable suddenly seemed to take it as a personal affront, when she answered, "But I brought my riding clothes all the way from New York to be photographed on a camel."

I tried to explain that I had not made this rule and urged her to please pass the word to all the ladies.

The next morning as we began assembling in the lobby Miss Phoenix raised her voice and said, "Look at Joan Fontaine, she's wearing slacks."

When I asked her if she had not informed Miss Fontaine, she answered, "Yes" and walked away in a huff.

I went after her and said, "Why don't you go change into your riding clothes. We'll wait for you." She wouldn't hear of it and all that day and for the next three days even when we took a boat trip up the Nile and visited the tomb, Miss Phoenix remained sullen and dejected.

Finally on the day we were to leave Cairo, a large bus had been ordered to take us back to Alexandria to rejoin the ship. I arrived at the bus a bit early and asked the driver if we went anywhere near the pyramids on our way to Alexandria. When he answered, "We go right by them" I called Miss Phoenix and commanded her to put on her riding clothes. Then I picked up a journalist and a photographer who were standing by, informed the bus driver that we were going on ahead, and to please be on the lookout for us at the pyramids.

I'm happy to say, we put Miss Phoenix on a camel, got the photographer to snap the picture and we met the bus on time. Miss Phoenix's mother received the photo, and everyone lived happily for the rest of the cruise.

We visited Bethlehem, and saw the manger where Christ was born, and later in Jerusalem, where He carried the cross, and to Mount Olive where He was crucified.

In Rome, Paul Newman and Joanne had to leave the cruise and fly home for a film committment. They were replaced by Patrice Munsel, her husband, Bob Schuler, two of my dearest friends, along with the cabaret star Bricktop. Brick, as she was affectionately known was an American negro, born in West Virginia, who became the toast of Paris in the twenties.

In front of the pyramids, pictured are: Joan Fontaine, Hugh O'Brian, Gloria Swanson, Ruth Ford and husband Zachary Scott and Nancy Cooke Jackson De Herrara, among others…

My loyal secretary, Vine Phoenix on the highest camel!

Sightseeing Greece: Paul Newman, Joanne Woodward & Joan Fontaine among others…

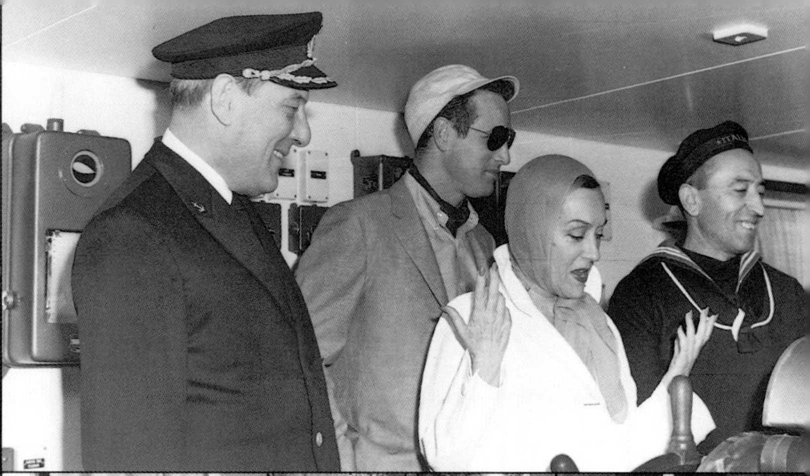

Aboard the
LEONARDO da VINCI

Pictured on the Celebrity Cruise are Gloria Swanson (as Charlie Chaplin),
Paul Newman, Joanne Woodward, Joan Fontaine & Patrice Munsel.

Cole Porter wrote a song "Miss Otis Regrets" for her and she made headlines by teaching the Prince of Wales the Blackbottom and the Charleston. T.S. Eliot put her in a poem and Fitzgerald, Hemingway and Waugh wrote about her. She was friend, entertainer, confidant and mother hen to all of them.

After the War, Bricktop moved to Rome and became a devout Catholic. Her memoirs were published in 1984 just before her death in New York. Her funeral was arranged by Duke Ellington's sister at St. Malachy Church on West 49th Street, sometimes known as the actor's chapel. I was asked to speak and I told the story that had happened a few years earlier in St. Patrick's Cathedral. It was Good Friday, during Holy Week and I had gone there for the three hour devotion. Bishop Fulton Sheean was officiating and he was such a brilliant and eloquent speaker that the three hours seemed like twenty minutes. As I stood up at the end to leave, I noticed for the first time the lady in black beside me. It was Bricktop. Neither of us had been aware of the others presence until that moment, as we had been so absorbed in Bishop Sheean's rhetoric. It was an emotional moment and we both fell into each others arms.

Bricktop

THE NINE O'CLOCKS
IX
OF NEW YORK

Chapter Eleven

The New York social scene is just one charity ball after another where one buys a ticket, makes a contribution and sits with the same group all evening. For sometime I thought New York should have an annual party like the famous "Dancing Class of Washington" where invitations were treated like state dinners at The White House.

When I had mentioned my idea to some of the Old Guard society, their immediate response was "Good idea, Earl. Let's do it!" It so happened that at a large party at the Fifth Avenue home of Anne Slater a great number of friends asked how the private club was coming. That evening, Harry Platt, Milton Holden, Martha Slater, Jane Hoving and I slipped away to a quiet adjoining room where definite rules were made with enthusiasm. A short time later, Pat Buckley,

Above: *Nan Kempner*

Top Right: *"You've all heard about the NINE O'CLOCKS. Haven't you? What? Well, it's a private New York club formed by Earl Blackwell and composed of 200 international socialites who think it's just marvelous to have a private party once a year just to dine and dance in internecine coziness…" writes SUZY in her noted NEW YORK POST syndicated column.*

Right: *Serge Obolensky*

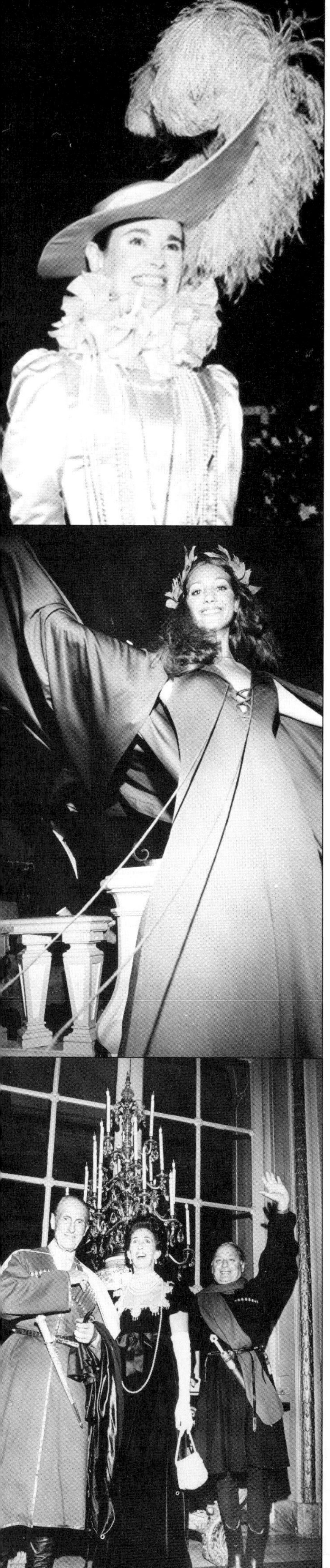

Noreen and John Drexel, and Candy and Jim Van Alen joined the board. Our plan was for the Nine O'Clocks to have friends come from all parts of the country and Europe, enjoying a relaxed evening of dancing and table hopping. There would be no table assignments or place cards so guests could move about freely and change places with each other. The first party at The Plaza Hotel was a costume ball called "The Turn of the Century" and it was an instant success with the founders forming a receiving line. Many of our annual parties centered around a main theme and guests were asked to dress accordingly.

One which I recall vividly was to honor Serge Obolensky's 88th birthday. The setting was St. Petersburg 1910 at the Winter Palace. The guests were requested to come dressed in costume for the gala; Serge was dressed in the same uniform he actually had worn as one of the Royal Guards.

Top Left: *Gloria Vanderbilt wearing a Hat that once belonged to her aunt, The Duchess of Marlborough*

Middle Left: *Marisa Berenson*

Bottom Left: *Mrs. John Drexel and Serge Obolensky*

Top Right: *Mr. & Mrs. Gil Shiva*

Middle Right: *Valerie Byfield and Betsy Bloomingdale*

Bottom Right: *Mr. & Mrs. Joshua Logan*

VOGUE'S NOTEBOOK

FLAPPER FLING

In New York, the Nine O'Clocks club winter dance always has a theme . . . this year: "Paris in the 1920s" . . . and it's fascinating to see what this urge to dress up brings out in people. Some get it and make it work to their advantage—a great beauty may become even more beautiful; a friend exhibits some rare facet of personality always hidden there, unsuspected. . . .

1. Josephine Kemp in black-and-white silk print by Ossie Clark. . . . **2.** Andrea Portago and Raymundo de Larrain might have stepped out of Rudolph Valentino's *Four Horsemen* in gleaming black-and-white costumes rented for the evening from Mme. Berthe. . . . **3.** Mrs. J. Gordon Douglas, junior, in violet velvet, cyclamen satin sash, and ropes of pearls. . . . **4.** Mrs. Alfred Bloomingdale in silver bugle beads, a touch of candy pink. . . . **5.** Joshua Logan impersonating a Paris taxi driver. . . . **6.** To many a memory, Bricktop was the twenties. She sang in a cabaret at the party in her Art Déco-pattern gold brocade. . . . **7.** The one and only Gloria Swanson, wearing diamond bracelets, circa 1929, from Cartier. . . . **8.** Mrs. Paul Manno dripping silver fringe. . . . **9.** Mrs. Thomas Kempner in a present-day Saint Laurent black sequin dress flashed with coral and gold, her sensational legs in sheer black stockings. . . . **10.** Earl Blackwell saw himself as Lucky Lindy. . . . **11.** Mrs. Michael Stone bought her costume at Bergdorf Goodman the day before— pretty brown chiffon by Harold Levine, and a black satin cloche. . . .

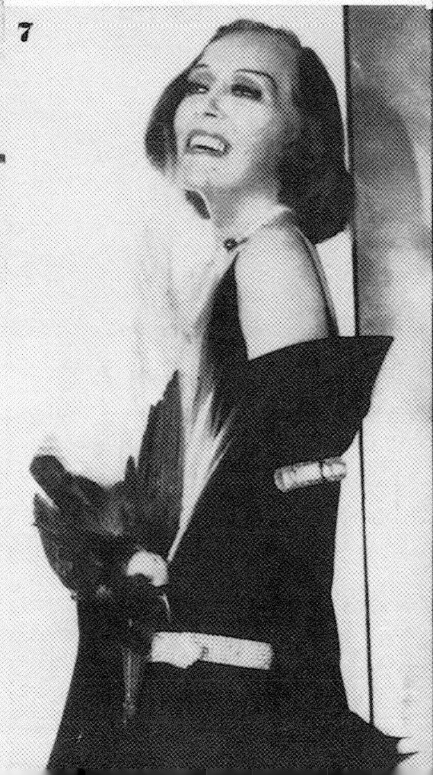

Opposite Page:

Top Row Left: *Frank Shields with Didi*

Top Row Middle: *Judy & Sam Peabody*

Top Row Right: *Jane Pickens Hoving*

Middle Row Left: *Pat Buckley*

Middle Row Center: *Sonny Whitney, Mary Lou Whitney, Michael Ballantine and Olivia De Havilland*

Bottom Row Left: *Winston & C.Z. Guest*

Bottom Row Right: *Arlene Francis & Kitty Carlisle Hart*

Right: *Mr. & Mrs. C.V. Whitney*

Below:
Mrs. Graham Mattison and Baron Alexis de Rede

Havin' a ball with Elizabeth Taylor wearing her Kabuki coiffure

Chapter Twelve

I've always loved Venice and from a casual remark, "Venice must be saved" made by Joseph Picone at a Night of Malta dinner, I dived in with my usual verve to create what the *London Times* labeled "The Party of the Century," and raised $500,000 for Venice.

I think one of the reasons we had such an outstanding success is that the guest list was extremely selective. I appointed a Chairman from each country, such as: Marella Agnelli from Italy, Jacqueline de Ribes from France, the Duchess of Alba from Spain and Clare Boothe Luce from the United States and when Suzy announced that each Chairman would be limited to only twenty-five invitations, everyone wanted to be there.

Richard Burton and Liz Taylor headed the list of notables who attended, along with Aristotle Onassis, Prince Rainier and Princess Grace of Monaco, Douglas Fairbanks, Jr., Dominique Zehrfuss, Count Bailey, Mrs. Clare Boothe Luce and Mrs. Joseph P. Kennedy.

The great Palace was aglow with lights and brilliant barges carried the guests to their party site. The theme of the ball was the 17th century and guests were so attired. Liz Taylor looked exquisite wearing a Kabuki coiffure from the film *Fusees* in which she starred with Richard Burton.

(left to right) *Behind the masks are: Rose Kennedy and Florence Vandercamp.*

Above: *Princess Grace came with two escorts dressed exactly alike.
One was Prince Rainier and the other his cousin.
She kept everyone guessing for most of the evening.*

Left: *Richard Burton, Elizabeth Taylor and Aristotle Onassis
at the Legendary Costume Ball at the Palazzo Rezzonico in Venice, 1967.*

Below: *Gore Vidal & Clare Boothe Luce*

RICHARD AVEDON

Embassy Ball Executive Chairmen

Mrs. Winston F. C. Guest, Vicomtesse de Ribes, Mrs. Thomas M. Bancroft, Jr.

Chapter Thirteen

One thing leads into another; that's how I got involved with all the Charity Balls. It all started when a young friend of mine, Gino di Grandi, the public relations head of several fashion accounts (one of them being the famous Fontana Sisters in Rome) organized a worldwide fashion tour of South America, North America and Europe. He arranged for Nancy Cooke Jackson (de Herrera) to present to each country an outfit representative of American fashions. They needed something special to climax the tour and asked me if I would organize an event to honor Cobina Wright, the Honorary Chairman and Nancy Cooke. I accepted with my usual drive and made it into a major event.

As a result of this initial success, I was asked to organize special events in Chicago, Houston, Atlanta, 3 great Embassy Balls in New York and the Love Party in Paris for Mary Wells Lawrence.

"The Love Party" 1969

Top Left: *At the Ambassador Ball the two lovely ladies beside me are:*
(left) Gene Tierney and (right) Cobina Wright

Above: *C. Z. Guest & Prince Philip*

Right: *The Duchess of Windsor with Judy Garland*
on their way to the Japanese Embassy Ball

Below: *Jacqueline de Ribes*

Bottom Right: *Lady Bird Johnson & Merle Oberon discuss the Embassy Ball.*

C. Z. Guest & Vicomtesse de Ribes

MARY WELLS LAWRENCE asked me to help her with the charity ball in Houston, Texas and this became the Crystal Ball. I said to her that we can reproduce the Crystal Palace and she said, "Who in the world can I get last minute?" I said, "Do you want Cecil Beaton?" and she said, "Yes!"

The next morning I flew to London and met with Cecil Beaton. The Crystal Ball was a big success with such people as President Lyndon Johnson attending the event.

Mary's husband, Harding Lawrence, President of Braniff Airlines, thanked me in a most unusual way. He gave me an International Airline Ticket which allowed me to fly anywhere, anytime for free. I wish I still had that card today!

Mary Wells Lawrence & Cecil Beaton

Princess Ghislaine de Polignac of Paris and Anne Slater of New York participating in an indoor bicycle race at the Sands Hotel in Las Vegas.

Sharing a happy moment with Donald and Ivana Trump at The Plaza Hotel in 1987; before their highly publicized divorce.

At a Plaza Hotel Ball; Pat & Bob Schuler

*Planning the Salute To Israel in 1973 are
Alan King, Thomas W. Phipps,
Ambassador Angier Biddle Duke and William J. Levitt.*

*"If we have a weakness, it's that too little accent has been placed on the cultural and social life of Israel," said Prime Minister, Golda Meir. So, the government hired me (on left)
to create a special 25th Anniversary Celebration in August 1973. Jerry Herman wrote a salute to Mrs. Meir and top performers from the U.S. (Patrice Munsel, Robert Merrill,
Arlene Dahl, Josephine Baker, Alan King) took part in the program. One of the most inspiring events of this "August Moon Weekend" (as it was called) was the appearance of
Rudolph Nureyev on opening night; he performed with the Royal Ballet in the Roman Amphitheater in Caesaria with the Mediterrannean as a backdrop.*

Chapter Fourteen

When I first went to Israel in 1962, I experienced the great joy of planting a tree near Haifa. On my return nine years later, I found a forest – and a nation that had grown along with my small sapling. One could not have been more impressed by this nation's vigor and courage – and the energy of its people.

Among the most energetic was Mira Avrech, the journalist, who to my great surprise told me she had followed my career with interest. She even made a point of saying she had attended a couple of international events I had coordinated – and caught me off guard by asking why I hadn't done one in her country. Wishing to be polite, I said I'd love to, never dreaming at the time that Mira's boundless enthusiasm for such a project would lead me on to the Salute to Israel weekend.

Over a period of 18 months I was bombarded with letters, cables and overseas calls urging me to come to Israel and get started. When business commitments prevented my doing so, Mira came to me. She arrived in New York in October of 1972, with government officials and the director of tourism – and her natural enthusiasm overflowing. We met over lunch with Bill Levitt and before we reached dessert, Bill had agreed to underwrite the initial expenses of the Salute to Israel celebrations, and serve as one of the chairmen.

The die was cast. I called in my associate, Tommy Phipps, who agreed to edit the Commemorative Album, and Clive David, the famed party architect, to execute the plans for the festivities in Israel.

Soon Angier Biddle Duke, former Ambassador to Spain and Chief of Protocol under Presidents Kennedy and Johnson, and Congressman Ogden Reid, former Ambassador to Israel, joined Bill as co-chairmen.

The committees started to form – Alan King agreed to assist with the entertainment, and Leo Greenland with the sponsorship of the Album. Clive David was off to Israel with Emmy Award-winning television producer Bill Angelos, who wanted to film the Salute to Israel as part of a wide-ranging TV tribute to the 25th Anniversary.

We were particularly fortunate in our endeavor – because our concept caught the eye and imagination of Prime Minister Golda Meir, who with her graciousness agreed that the entire weekend could be held "in her presence!"

(left to right) William & Simone Levitt with Golda Meir

Chapter Fifteen

Eugenia Sheppard and I go back to our first meeting on Charles Revson's luxurious yacht, the Ultima II. For seven summers both of us were invited by Charles and Lyn to sail all over the Mediterranean. We always boarded the first day of August in Monte Carlo, and after a few days there, usually to attend the Red Cross Gala with Princess Grace, we would sail off to Majorca, to Spain, to Sardenia or the Greek Islands, then to Turkey and Israel and finally to Venice. It was a wonderful adventure.

Charles was an extremely thoughtful and generous host. At each port, he would arrange to have two limousines waiting to take us wherever we wished to go. However, he kept the temperature on board unbelievably cold. In the evenings after dinner, we would go down to the main salon to watch a movie. Even with a sweater on, Eugenia would wrap herself in a blanket and sit on the floor. She looked like a teddy bear and I just had to hug her. It was the beginning of our close relationship that lasted to her death some twelve years later.

After Lyn and Charles separated, Eugenia and I spent our summers at my home in the Bahamas, where we wrote our three novels together. In 1971, I had just completed my home in the Bahamas; Eugenia along with Jim and Tommy Tailer and Budd Calisch were my first house guests. Eugenia fell in love with the house which I had named CARRIEARL after my mother and father.

It was amazing to see a sudden change in Eugenia. She suddenly became another person. Instead of poking away at her portable typewriter, Eugenia was standing in the kitchen making corn muffins.

In my Bahamian home, there was no telephone; very little social life. All that time there was only one telephone on the *entire* island. This is why we started work on our novels. The first one was *Crystal Clear.* We didn't tell anyone about it until we were halfway through when I suggested to Eugenia that we should get some reactions so we know if we're on the right track. We sent the first nine chapters to Swifty Lazar, one of the top literary agents, to get his reaction. He responded immediately and said he liked it and when it was finished he would like to represent us. I'll never forget the day I received a call from Sandy Richardson from Doubleday saying he heard we were writing a novel and he would like to read it.

In the afternoon I took it over personally and handed it to Richardson's secretary. After working on it for nine to ten months I wasn't about to trust a messenger with the manuscript. The next morning I had a call from Richardson. He said he only started reading it after dinner but didn't put it down until he finished it. Doubleday said they would like to publish it. I barely managed to speak, I was so shocked. I told them to contact our agent, Swifty Lazar. I couldn't

MISTER CELEBRITY

wait to telephone Eugenia. When I finally reached her and relayed the exciting news she said, "I'm going to faint."

Eugenia and I were inseparable. One day Gaylord Hauser called on the telephone and said he would like to bring Greta Garbo for tea. My first instinct was to call Eugenia, but knowing Garbo's dislike for the press I was concerned. I needn't have been because the minute Eugenia appeared Garbo stood up and hugged her and said, "Why you're just a little doll." Doll is a word many people used in describing Eugenia, with her small frame, blonde ringlets and cornflower blue eyes.

Though not one to mince words, once in Paris, covering the French collections, she attended the Yves.St. Laurent show. She wrote, "There's only one word to describe the Laurent collection, 'hideous'." Still, the Parisian designers spoke admiringly of her. "One of the best fashion journalists," said Marc Bohan of Christian Dior. "When she didn't like something, she explained why, and it made sense." When Eugenia, by chance, discovered Grace Kelly was buying yellow lingerie for her trousseau; she decided to establish the first fashion-oriented gossip column called "Inside Fashion."

Carol Channing
"The book was an eye-opener—and my eyes are already pretty big."
& Suzy
"I liked it. I really liked it."
& Gaylord Hauser
"I was captivated. Crystal is an extraordinary woman."
& Peter Duchin
"An exciting book. Once started, it's impossible to put down."
& Angie Dickenson
"Crystal is a glamourous career woman with spunk. I would love to play Crystal in the movie."
have all fallen in love with
Crystal Clear
by Eugenia Sheppard & Earl Blackwell
Only two people who know everybody could have created CRYSTAL CLEAR—the novel that takes you inside the closely-guarded world where the super-celebrities of business, fashion, society and show business live and love.
$10.00 at all booksellers
DOUBLEDAY

MISTER CELEBRITY

Chapter Sixteen

I had known Grace Kelly for some time and was very happy to be invited to her wedding in Monaco. The papers were full of news stories each day and there was great excitement about the beautiful American movie star marrying a Royal Prince. Before leaving, I went to the Monaco embassy in New York and got an official photograph of Grace and Rainier, then I had postcards made. On the plane going over I addressed them to the girls in my office and to my

Aug. 7th
1978

Dear Earl —

Many thanks to you and Eugenie for sending me your book "Crystal clear" via Millie — I am delighted to have it and do look forward to reading it this summer — My congratulations to you both on your wonderful success — sorry not to see you this summer —

Affectionate regards
Grace

— 89 —

plumber, the dry cleaner, the grocer—not my social friends. On the day of the wedding I went to the post office in Monte Carlo and obtained the official postmark of that memorable day and sent the card off. To this day I get thanks over and over again.

I'll never forget the church the day of the wedding and seeing Grace walk down the aisle. Her skin was like alabaster-marble. Dorothy Kilgallen was sitting in front of me and just as Grace walked down the aisle and reached the altar, Dorothy fainted.

I was terribly worried about her—we all were. She was carried out of the church. Afterwards, as I walked out of the church, the ceremony having ended, there was a plumbing shop across the way. I noticed it because I saw Dorothy inside. She was on the phone to New York, the first to file her story on the wedding. Dorothy was quite a reporter. She had only pretended to faint.

Princess Grace and I maintained our friendship through the years. Our last meeting was at the Theater Hall of Fame ceremony which I organized at the Gershwin Theater in 1981. Grace's uncle, the playwright George Kelly, had been elected to the Hall of Fame that year, and Grace was there to accept the award in his behalf.

Princess Grace accepting the award for her uncle, playwright George Kelly at the Theater Hall of Fame, 1981.

with Marilyn Monroe at JFK Birthday Party, May 1962

Chapter Seventeen

I was asked to assist with President Kennedy's birthday party at Madison Square Garden. My duty was to invite celebrities to appear. Jack Benny and Jimmy Durante were there. Maria Callas came from Paris. When I called Marilyn in Hollywood and asked her if she'd come sing "Happy Birthday, Mr. President," her first question was "Is Bobby Going to be there?"

Obviously, she had a school girl crush on him before she ever met him. After the big celebration at Madison Square Garden, there was a small intimate dinner given at the Manhattan town house of Matilde and Arthur Krim. That was where Marilyn met Bobby for the very first time. They sat together in a corner and laughed and joked all night. It was the beginning of their friendship. Many photographs were taken that evening of Marilyn with the President and also with Bobby, but I later learned that orders from the White House said they must be destroyed.

Following the President's Birthday celebration at Madison Square Garden, there was a private reception.
Pictured: (l-r) President Kennedy, me, Adlai Stevenson and Maria Callas.

Merle Oberon

Below: *In Istanbul; (left to right) Sloan Simpson,
Miguel Lopez-Lecube, Merle Oberon,
Walter Troutman and Millie Considine.*

Chapter Eighteen

Merle Oberon had only one short scene in Alexander Korda's film *The Private Lives of Henry III* when as Anne Boylen on the way to the guillotine she said, "It's such a little neck," but it brought her instant stardom…Korda changed her name from Merle O'Brian Thompson to Merle Oberon and after their marriage, when her husband was knighted, she became Lady Korda.

Merle later married Lucien Ballard in Hollywood but it was after her second divorce that our paths crossed for the first time in Madrid, the summer of 1953, at the opening of the Castelana Hilton Hotel. It was a star studded event with guests like Gary Cooper, Bill Hearst, Jinx Falkenberg, Sloan Simpson, Mary Martin, Millie and Bob Considine, Rosemary and Earl Wilson and Maggi and Jim Nolan, etc. Maggi later became the director of the Paris bureau. I remember accompanying Merle to a bullfight, my very first, and it was exciting…

After Madrid, came the opening of the Nile Hilton in Cairo followed by the Istanbul Hilton's personal guest list. In Istanbul, I remember taking a boat trip up the Bostras with Merle and William Randolph Hearst, Jr. We visited a beautiful Turkish Palace along the way with Bill Hearst commenting, "I'm glad Dad missed this one or it would be on a mountain top in California."

In December 1966 I received an invitation from Conrad Hilton to attend the opening of still another hotel, this one in Mexico City. When I checked my calendar I discovered, much to my chagrin, a conflict. I had been booked to give a lecture at the University of Alabama followed by one in Atlanta. I was frantically trying to reschedule these two dates when I had a call from Merle. She was passing through New York and staying at the Park Lane. She asked if I was going to the Mexico opening and when I said I wasn't sure, she said, "Well, if you don't go, I won't go."

Fortunately, I succeeded in changing the dates of my lecture and was able to accompany Merle to Mexico. Little did either of us realize the consequences. On the very first night in Mexico City she met Bruno Pagliai and it changed her whole life, and his, too.

Bill & Simone Levitt

Chapter Nineteen

I was very fond of Charles Revson. I'm sure some people thought I was on his payroll, as a public relations consultant, but I never received a penny from him. However, William Levitt, the builder who created Levittown, assumed I was working for Charles. When he and his lovely wife, Simone, purchased a yacht even larger than Charles', calling it "LA BELLE SIMONE," he engaged me as his p.r. consultant for an astronomical fifty thousand dollars a year. Perhaps now it doesn't seem so great a figure, but it was unheard of just fifteen years ago. There was a huge rivalry between these two tycoons, and how I managed to keep both friendships through the years could fill a chapter or two.

Bill and Simone Levitt were marvelous hosts. There were four chefs (French, Chinese, Italian, Mexican) and a crew of 33 aboard LA BELLE SIMONE. Following dinner in the Grand Salon, Bill would entertain his guests by accompanying them at the piano. They were all expected to contribute something to the festivities - a joke, a song, a poem - a performance of some kind, and since some of his guests had great voices like Patrice Munsel and were great humorists like Alan King, the impromptu entertainment was never dull.

One Summer, Simone and Bill began the annual Summer cruise from London where LA BELLE SIMONE was anchored in the Thames. There was something very special about boarding in London knowing we were going to sail past Gibraltor and stop in Spain enroute to Monte Carlo.

The night before we sailed, Simone and Bill gave a large party and among the guests were Lily Palmer, Rex Harrison, the Duchess of Argyle, Nancy Holmes, John Galliher and Pauline Trigére. When we arrived in Marbella, Spain, the first person to catch our eye was an attractive woman, standing on the very tip of the dock waving. As we came closer, I borrowed a telescope, I recognized the woman who was still waving frantically. I yelled it was "Honey," meaning Princess Hohenlohe, the former Honeychild Wilder. As we approached the harbour we soon realized LA BELLE SIMONE was too

Aboard La Belle Simone: *Celebrating Shirley Lord's Wedding*

Above: *Michael York visits La Belle Simone*

Below: *with Simone Levitt*

large to enter, and therefore we anchored
outside the harbour, and had to take a small
motor dingy ashore. By that time, Honey had
a mass of friends waiting to welcome us.
Among them, Terry and Hubert Pantz, Aline

and Luis Romanones and Jan Neff.

The next day there must have been
thirty guests on board LA BELLE SIMONE
for the luncheon. As we stood sipping
cocktails around the pool before lunch, the
most embarrassing thing that ever happened
to me occurred. We heard a splash and
looked to see that Bill Levitt had fallen into
the pool. As I turned to view, someone
pushed me and I went splashing into the
pool. I was all dressed for the party and as I
came up for air, I heard screams of laughter
and realized the hairpiece I had been
wearing had washed away.

That same Summer, both the Revson
and Levitt yachts were docked right next to
each other at Monte Carlo and that was a
nightmare to be in the middle of the friction
between these two mighty men.

Charles Revson was a thoughtful host.
Every port we stopped he would have two
limousines with a bi-lingual driver waiting
to take us wherever we wanted to go.
However, he had a number of idiosyncricies;
one of them was never telling us what part
of the world we were going to visit. After
Monte Carlo, he would keep our destination
as a secret. We would often find ourselves
guessing if we turned right it would be Spain
and Tangiers, or left would be the Greek
Islands or Israel. He always had Dr. Alfred
Steiner aboard and a chef who knew favorite
recipes of all his guests.

Charles Revson was also quite
stubborn. He would always get his way. On

some nights on his boat, Lyn would read a list of films she had brought on board and then asked for a vote on which film we would like to see. Nobody wanted to see a western; nobody except Charles. So we would always see the westerns no matter what the vote.

In his handsome New York duplex he arranged the luxurious dining room as if it were on board his ship, with 24 chairs surrounding the dining table all fastened to the floor with brass screws. A novel idea, but he was told it was better to be flexible, and not to always have to seat 24 guests at each dinner. He refused to change his mind.

As a consequence, so many times I

Lyn Revson at Nine O'Clocks

received frantic calls from Lyn saying that two of her dinner guests that evening were detained out-of-town, or were suddenly taken ill, and could I possibly think of a good substitute.

Eugenia Sheppard and I were invited to the Revson's tenth wedding anniversary party. It was held on a Saturday night at their country home near White Plains. It was a festive evening and besides glamourous jewelry, one of Charles' presents to Lyn was a tin box with ten one-thousand dollar bills.

Lyn and Charles drove back to town on Sunday night and Monday morning, after breakfast, Charles kissed Lyn on the cheek and headed for his office, as he had done so many weekday mornings during their decade of marriage. An hour later, Lyn received a telephone call from Charles' attorney. He announced to a startled Lyn that Mr. Revson would not be returning. He would send for his clothes and immediately start divorce proceedings. Lyn was in shock for almost a year.

Chapter Twenty

Olivia De Havilland once said to me, "Earl, you are a very lucky fellow. I think your great success is due to the fact that you've been in the right place at the right time, and asked the right questions to the right people."

I have been lucky, there is no doubt about it. A good example is the way I found my palatial New York Penthouse. I was on a train going from Rome to Venice when a stranger sat down in the seat next to me, and started to speak Italian. I apologized in English, saying only a few words in Italian.

We soon discovered that we were both from New York. He was an attorney, with offices on Wall Street and it took a long time describing Celebrity Service. When we arrived in Venice we exchanged business cards. A couple of months later, I had a telephone call. "Earl Blackwell this is Joe Cardillo. Remember, we met on the train to Venice? You told me about Celebrity Service, and now I am looking for a celebrity and hope you can assist me."

He gave me the name of the celebrity whose whereabouts he was seeking, and I was able to furnish the current address in South America.

A few weeks later, while lunching at the Russian Tea Room, I ran into Cardillo and, before I could ask if he had found the celebrity he was looking for, he said, "Thanks to Celebrity Service my great problem was solved." He then continued, "You see, I represent an apartment building

Emanuel Ax entertained a select group of guests in my ballroom. Included are: Salvador Dali, Anne Slater, Cleveland Amory, among others…

on 57th Street, just across the street, and this well known person had leased the Penthouse, bringing in artists to paint murals in the Ballroom." He never occupied the apartment and was seven months in arrears with his rent, so the apartment was put back on the market. I asked Cardillo if I could go after lunch to see it. We did and the moment we opened the door to the ballroom, I knew it had to be mine and I took it over immediately.

Moving from a three-room apartment into a twelve room penthouse was quite a challenge but I took my time furnishing and decorating each room. I had been around the world and collected oriental art along with two hand-carved Chinese lamps that started the library.

Anita Vanderbilt was one of my first guests and when she saw my enormous terrace, without a chair or bench to sit on, she exclaimed, "I have the perfect house present for you, Earl. I had a lovely terrace in my last apartment. I had over 18 pieces that were especially designed wrought iron furniture. They are in storage and I will arrange tomorrow to have them sent here to you."

The Penthouse was slowly taking shape. There was only one problem – someone to run the house, supervise the cleaning, order the food for the household, etc. The first person I interviewed from the Agency was a man from Poland. He came with his nine year old son, Emanuel, who had just won a scholarship to Juillard. We went over the duties that were needed. I asked his young son to play something on my piano and he did so brilliantly. Everything was agreed upon and he asked when he could move in and I said "today if you wish." The father, Joachim was a strict disciplinarian and had his son practice two hours in the morning before going to school and four hours after school. All went well until Joachim became ill and I arranged for him to go to the City of Hope Hospital in Los Angeles. At the same time I arranged for Emanuel's mother – who had stayed behind in Canada to work – to come live with us and take care of Emanuel.

Hellen Ax had suffered terribly during the war. At one point she was in the firing line in Poland to be shot any moment, when a German officer said, "take that small woman on the end out – she is a good cook – we need her."

After a couple of months Joachim came back and soon found a position on the faculty of a Connecticut College.

Maureen O'Sullivan, an old and dear friend ever since my days at MGM in Hollywood, called to say she was on her way over to see an apartment that had just become available in my building. I told her I would meet her in the lobby and we would have a chance for a short visit.

We were shown the third floor apartment that had once belonged to Ely Culbertson.

Emanuel and his mother Hellen Ax

Actually, there were two apartments, one medium size, with two bedrooms, and another very small one.

I could tell at once that the third floor apartment was not right for Maureen, who had her daughter Mia living with her at that time. However, I've always been interested in architecture and the thought of removing a wall and turning the two apartments into one, intrigued me. When I returned to the Penthouse, I started describing to Miss Phoenix the two apartments they were going to make into one. Joachim Ax, who had been sitting next to the window, overheard me and said, "Mr. Blackwell, what about us?"

I had realized for some time that with Emanuel now a teenager, the two attic rooms were no longer suitable for a family of three. "But Joachim," I answered, "You couldn't afford the rent. It would be more than Fifteen Hundred Dollars a month." As I spoke, I thought of an idea. The Ax Family could live in one apartment while renting the other completely furnished in order to pay for both apartments. I could ask all my friends if they had a lamp, chair, or desk that they were not using to give to my friends.

I turned to Miss Phoenix and said, "Get me John Avalon of the Realty firm." When his office answered, I spoke quickly: "I want to rent the apartment on the third floor."

"It's been rented, Mr. Blackwell," they replied. "No, it has not," I stated matter-of-factly. "I saw it only five minutes ago." They clarified, "We already have a check for deposit."

"Then tear it up," I insisted. "I am on my way down to your office. This family I want the apartment for have suffered under the Germans, the Russians, and have a son who is a genius. I will guarantee the rent."

I got the apartment and some time later my attorney said, "Why don't you like Barbara Walters?" "What do you mean?" I asked. "I don't know her, but I like her very much on television." He replied with a surprise. "She thinks you hate her. You took the apartment away from her!"

I was never told who had made the deposit on the apartment and informed the lawyer for the building. "Please assure Ms. Walters that she will definately get the next apartment which becomes available." Luckily, a short time later a much larger apartment in the front of the building on the fifth floor opened up and Barbara lived there for ten years. After Barbara moved to Park Avenue, Eugenia Sheppard lived there for six years.

As we all know, Emanuel Ax has become one of the great pianists of our time. Compared to Rubinstein and others of world fame, his career has flourished even more than we ever imagined. Noted not only for his international solo performances, Emanuel has appeared with chamber groups, including acclaimed concerts with violinist Young-Uck Kim and cellist Yo-Yo Ma. Hellen Ax still reminisces about standing on my terrace overlooking 57th Street and hoping, "Could it be, one day, my son will play Carnegie Hall?" Emanuel has performed at Carnegie Hall dozens of times.

Emanuel Ax

Uris theatre
Theater
HALL of
FAME

Chapter Twenty-One

One day, I was having lunch at Gallagher's and sitting at the next table were two very good friends, James Nederlander and Gerard Oestreicher. After lunch, as I started to leave Jimmy said to me, "Sit with us a minute." Then he and Gerard Oestreicher told me that they were building the largest theatre on Broadway. They said it would be called the URIS Theater after the Real Estate tycoon. He said, "Earl, you're always creating such special events around the world. Why don't you think of something for our new theatre that will have enormous lobby space." The next day, I called Jimmy and said I had the perfect vehicle... The Theater Hall of Fame... which would honor the greats of the American Theatre. Without hesitating, he said, "This space is yours, Earl. Go ahead."

I first called Arnold Weissberger who was in complete accord with my idea and immediately incorporated a format. To be eligible for membership in the Theater Hall of Fame, a notable must have had a career spanning at least 25 years on Broadway and with more than five major credits. The Drama Editors and Drama Critics vote annually on who would be honored.

A year later, 1971, John Lindsay (the mayor of New York) officiated at the formal opening ceremony when 25 Greats from Maude Adams to Florenz Ziegfeld were inducted. It was a joy to see Fred and Adele Astaire together, along with Oscar Hammerstein and Richard Rodgers.

Ralph Alswang, Joshua Logan, Helen Hayes, Anita Loos, and Gerard Oestricher join me on a tour of the future URIS THEATER (Fall/1971). The theatre was later renamed the Gershwin Theater which displays the Theater Hall of Fame Awards.

Clare Boothe Luce and producer Frederick Brisson inspect the under-construction URIS THEATER.

Top Left: *with Patrice Munsel and Tommy Tune*

Middle Left: *Ethel Merman & Carol Channing*

Bottom Left: *my sister Mary celebrates with me*

Below: *Producer David Merrick*

Opposite Page
Top Left: *Lillian Gish*
Top Right: *Helen Hayes & Richard Burton*
Middle Right: *Backstage at the Gershwin: (Seated left to right)
Joanne Woodward, Geraldine Fitzgerald,
Douglas Fairbanks, Jr. and Pamela Harriman*
Bottom Left: *Kate Burton*
Bottom Right: *Lucille Lortel with Sidney Kingsley*
(Photos: Anthony Mauer)

Fred Astaire (Photo: R. Deutsch)

Neil Simon & Maureen Stapleton (Photo: Anthony Mauer)

Top Left: *Celebrating at Sardi's:*
John Kander & Fred Ebb with Liza Minnelli
after the 1991 ceremony.

Above: *Dorothy Hammerstein* (Photo: Sam Ross)

Top Right: *Diana Ross came to a ceremony*

Bottom Right: *Fred & Adele Astaire*
presented with a scroll by John Lindsay
(Photo: Wagner International)

Al Pacino & Grace Kelly
(Photo: Anthony Mauer)

Ray Bolger & Lillian Gish were inducted.

Chita Rivera & her daughter

Ethel Merman inducted into
the THEATRE HALL OF FAME,
along with Frederic March (left)
and Fred Astaire (center rear)

Above
At Sardi's with good friends Douglas Fairbanks, Jr and Arlene Dahl

Top Right
Jerry Herman & Arlene Francis

Bottom Right
Tommy Tune as he is inducted into the
THEATER HALL OF FAME 1991

Below
Bernadette Peters & James Earl Jones

(Photos: Anthony Mauer)

Helen Hayes

Douglas Fairbanks, Jr. presented me with the honor of being inducted into the Theater Hall of Fame (February 1991).

February 27, 1991

Dear Earl,

I was heart sick to miss your day at the Gershwin. It was the speech I had wanted to make more then any for the past few years. I comforted myself in the hospital bed by saying it soto voce for my own amazement.

"This is an especially happy occasion for all of us who have benefited from the friendship of Earl Blackwell. He has given us a permanent place in theatre history and he belongs right there where he put us, making sure that we do not skip away into obscurity"

There was more than that, but it does not read as well as it speaks.

Thank you dear Earl for all that you have done for me and for our beloved theatre. Keep well.

Devotedly

Helen Hayes

Chapter Twenty-Two

THE DUKE OF WINDSOR

I was always elated to be in the presence of his Royal Highness... The Duke of Windsor. During his youth he traveled all over the world as the admitted "First salesman of the British Empire." He was Prince Charming, arbiter of fashion and incredibly popular. He was given a ticker tape parade up Broadway on his first visit to America in 1919, followed by a ball given in his honor by Mrs. Whitelaw Reid. He was back again in 1924 to watch the international polo matches at Meadowbrook. American society adopted him as its own Crown Prince and he was given a merry round of parties. There was even a song at the time, "I danced with the man, Who danced with the girl, Who danced with the Prince of Wales."

The first time I visited the Duke and Duchess of Windsor at their home in Neuilly, just outside of Paris I noticed a huge woven tapestry, a sort of map, hanging on the wall in their library. I asked the Duke what the significance of it was and he explained, "These are all the places I visited when I was Prince of Wales.

It was never easy for him having made the decision to abdicate, but he truly loved Wallis Simpson, the American divorcee, so very much. There was always a melancholy look on his face, although he might have projected that upon him. However, I like to think he died thinking it was all worthwhile.

I can recall very vividly the time of the abdication. The papers had been full of his love affair with Wallis Simpson and the problem with the Prime Minister Stanley Baldwin. It was mid-December 1936. I was driving from California to Atlanta to spend Christmas with my family. While crossing the desert, I pulled off the road and turned on the radio in the car to hear the King of England make his farewell speech. I am quite sure that anyone who heard it will never forget it. He started by saying: "At long last I am able to say a few words on my own..."

Little did I ever dream, sitting there listening to the King of England giving up his throne, that one day I would know him, and the lady who brought this all about.

One year in Paris, I was invited to dinner at the home of Antenor and Beatrix Patino. It was a small but very elegant dinner party with about twelve guests. The Duke of Windsor was sitting just opposite me and I watched him take distinct notice of the dinner plates, which he admired... He turned his plate over and then said, "Yes, I thought so. You see, they used to be mine."

THE DUCHESS OF WINDSOR

At the time of the Duke's death in 1972, the photograph of the tragic, yet noble face of the widowed Duchess of Windsor, glancing out from a heavily curtained window of Buckingham Palace, will never be erased from my memory. It signaled the end of the Love Story of the Century.

For a while after the Duke's death, the Duchess continued to see her close friends and

It was December 1936 when I was driving East that I pulled over to the
side of the road and heard the abdication of King Edward VIII on the radio.
Pictured: The Duke & Duchess of Windsor

Duchess of Windsor (Photo: Sheppard)

make her annual visit to New York. I always saw her when she was in town and on one visit in the mid-seventies arranged a small dinner party in her honor the night before she returned to France. Little did any of us know that evening that it would be her last on American soil. A few months later she became ill, then a recluse, and none of her very close friends could reach her. It was sad to think that this once witty and sparkling woman would spend the last years of her life in complete isolation.

Duchess of Windsor (2nd from left) pictured here with Carroll Petrie, Judy Garland & Cordelia Biddle Robertson

Ginger Rogers

Chapter Twenty-Three

Oneday, while waiting in the lobby of the George V for two friends, Budd Calisch and Peggy Fears, I picked up the *Herald Tribune* and was glancing through it when I saw a small item that caught my eye. It said: "Ginger Rogers is headed for Paris aboard the Liberte."

I decided on the spur of the moment to send a cable to the ship asking her to dine with me on her first night in Paris. I wasn't sure Ginger would remember me. We had met once in New York through her cousin, Phyllis Frazier Wagner, and briefly in Palm Springs at a tennis game. Obviously, she did for the next day I received a message saying, "I accept with pleasure. Call me at the Meurice."

Ginger was radiant that night when we dined at Maxim's and afterwards went to a big gala at Elsa Schiaparelli's home. That was the beginning of a wonderful friendship. Ginger and I were together every night in Paris – attending Jacques Fath's costume ball, and Elsa Maxwell's dance and so forth.... At one of the parties she met a handsome young man, Jacques Bergerac. Although he was at least ten years younger than her, she fell madly in love with him.

When Jacques had to go down to Monte Carlo on business, Ginger and I went down two nights later. My very good friend, Anita Colby (who had been the top model in New York and called "The Face") joined us one night for a drive over to Italy for a special dinner. Ginger and Jacques were in the front seat while Anita and I sat in the back. When we reached the border, to check out our passports, I was impressed with Ginger; instead of hiding her age, she opened her purse and handed Jacques her passport.

When it was time to return to Paris for Monte Carlo, Jacques had to go on ahead by plane; Ginger and I decided to drive. During the long trip, we talked about many things, one of them was Religion. She has always been a profound Christian Scientist and asked my thoughts on certain beliefs. She was surprised to learn that I shared many of her views. That trip cemented our relationship which has lasted all these years.

Jacques and Ginger were married four months later. I had a wedding party for them in New York and I tried to get small miniature brides for every table. I searched all over Manhattan to find a blonde bride and discovered they don't exist. I ended up buying some yellow paint and painting them blonde myself. Unfortunately, their marriage didn't last very long, and neither did Jacques' career as an actor. His only important film role was in *Gigi*, where he played the part of a gigilo with Eva Gabor.

Jacques' four year marriage to Dorothy Malone produced two children, Mimi and Diane. After their divorce, Jacques wanted to take his two daughters to France for Summer Vacation to visit his mother. Jacques was staying with me in New York anxiously waiting for the children to arrive. When they finally arrived a day late, they had no baggage whatsoever. All

With good friends, Anita Colby, Ginger Rogers & Jacques Bergerac

…Dancing with Ginger Rogers

Ginger & me in Monte Carlo

Paris, 1953. A night out with Ginger Rogers and Orson Welles at Jacques Fath's costume ball.

they had was what they were wearing: cotton dresses and sneakers. This meant Jacques had to take the girls on a shopping spree which Dorothy Malone had purposely planned.

Another summer when Jacques was staying with me, I invited Lyn and Charles Revson for dinner; it was Basille Day. Charles said, "Jacques, what are you doing these days?" He said, "I've given up Hollywood and I'm returning to France to start my career all over." Charles replied, "Come and see me tomorrow." As a result, Jacques went to work for Revlon beginning as a salesman at Bamberger's in Brooklyn and ended up as the President of Revlon in France and his brother, Michel, became President of Revlon in New York.

Chapter Twenty-Four

Although I had known and admired Anita Loos for a long time, it was not until I moved into my penthouse on West 57th Street that we became neighbors and very close friends.

At the age of twelve, Anita produced her first scenario, then went on to become one of Hollywood's first women screen-writers and one of its most successful. Then came "Gentlemen Prefer Blondes," which she wrote in 1925 for *Harper's Bazaar.* It may not have proved that diamonds are a girl's best friend, but they certainly were a good investment for Anita. After its first publication, it was subsequently made into a Broadway comedy, then a movie, and two musicals besides being translated into 13 languages.

I remember when Gilbert Miller produced the Broadway comedy "GIGI," Anita's adaption of Colettes original story. The leading role of "GIGI" was played by Audrey Hepburn, a charming young actress that I had recently met through Gloria Swanson's daughter. I was invited to the first night and was part of the ovation given to Audrey at the final curtain. The next day when Gilbert Miller decided to place Audrey's name above the title, thus making her a Broadway star, I sent a cameraman over to photograph the marquis. Then sent the finished photo to Audrey.

Audrey thanked me profusely saying, "The picture you sent me Earl meant more than you'll ever know because when I told my mother in Belgium my exciting news, she didn't quite comprehend what I was saying, but now with your thoughtful photograph, she will see that I've really become a Broadway star."

Anita Loos & Audrey Hepburn

Audrey Hepburn

Above: *Eva Gabor*

Right: *Zsa Zsa Gabor is full of smiles; she's listed in the first CELEBRITY REGISTER!*

Chapter Twenty-Five

ZSA ZSA GABOR

Late one afternoon, I was driving from Cannes to Monte Carlo and decided to spend the night in Nice at the Hotel Negresco. Early the next morning I had a telephone call from a photographer I had met at the Film Festival and I asked, "How in the world did you know where I was?" He replied, "I happened to be passing the hotel last night when you drove in." He added, "I thought you'd like to know GARBO arrived last night at the Hotel St. Vence and maybe you want to call her." "I wouldn't dare," I replied. "I don't know her that well." But he insisted, "You were with her everyday at the Film Festival." I said, "Oh, you mean GABOR...Zsa Zsa GABOR." He agreed, "Yes, she arrived last night with Rubirosa." I thanked him and said I'll call and say hello. When I got Zsa Zsa on the phone she said, "My God, Earl. Do you have spies everywhere? How did you know I was here?" This conversation resulted in our having lunch together and Porfirio Rubirosa becoming a good friend.

As we all know, although Rubirosa married Barbara Hutton, he continued his relationship with Zsa Zsa. One time, during this brief marriage to Barbara, I was having dinner with them at the Moulin Rouge in Palm Beach. At the end of the meal Barbara asked to borrow a pen. I reached into my jacket and without thinking, handed her one. It was in mid-air that I realized the pen had been a present from Zsa Zsa and was imprinted with the words: "With the compliments of Zsa Zsa Gabor." Was my face red!

My favorite story about Zsa Zsa is when she once remarked: "I'm a very good housekeeper. Everytime I get a divorce, I keep the house."

EVA GABOR

At my 50th Anniversary Party Eva Gabor stood up and, unrehearsed, took over the microphone and told of our first meeting, shortly after her arrival in America. In telling how our friendship has flourished these many years, she described the early days when we were so broke that our lunch often meant cutting one sandwich into two parts. Then to another extreme, we happened to be in London at the same time and were invited to Marlene Dietrich's opening night at the Kit Kat Club. A table for two was placed in the center of the first row and Noel Coward as the Master of Ceremonies acknowledged us by saying: "A special welcome to my favorite American friends, "EVA GABOR and EARL BLACKWELL."

Eva Gabor & Robert Schuler

Earl dear —
Your friendship has meant
so much to me over the years.
With admiration and love, Arlene

Chapter Twenty-Six

Arlene Dahl has an inner beauty which equals her perfect photogenic face. I attended her first wedding to Lex Barker, all the way thru to her seventh marriage to Marc Rosen.

Arlene has never said "No" to me. At the 25th Anniversary party for Golda Meir she sang and entertained. At my recent Birthday party at The Mark Hotel she was the Mistress of Ceremony. Her voice is pure magic. When I invite her to be a part of any event in the world – she's always there for me ...

Arlene Dahl and Rock Hudson

Arlene Dahl and her husband, at the time, Fernando Lamas, join my father for dinner.

Ann Miller

Chapter Twenty-Seven

An old friend from MGM, Ann Miller, was touring the country in SUGAR BABIES with Mickey Rooney. At a restaurant one evening, she shouted across the room to me — "You LIED about my age...I'm not that old!" We looked her up the next day in the CELEBRITY REGISTER and discovered that if I had used the date she wanted, she would have been married at 12!

On a Hilton Junket to Trinidad (right to left); Ann Miller, a Hollywood Dance Director, Millie Considine, Virginia Warren and me.

Chapter Twenty-Eight

Two of my dearest friends are Bob Schuler and his wife, Patrice Munsel. Patrice made her musical debut at 17 as the youngest soprano of the Metropolitan Opera.

On a trip to visit me in the Bahamas, Pat naturally brought along her well-known oversized hat collection. When it came time for Pat and Bob to return to New York, Pat purposedly forgot one of her hats — an enormously brimmed one. She suggested I could have a lot of fun with this by letting Eugenia Sheppard model it. Indeed, she was right. When tiny Eugenia placed it atop her head, she actually disappeared from sight. She looked like a pretty toadstool!

Bob Schuler and Patrice Munsel recently celebrated their 39th Wedding Anniversary. They radiate happiness and it is a joy to be with them.

Pat & Bob Schuler

Patrice Munsel

Wendy Carduna & Porter Ijams

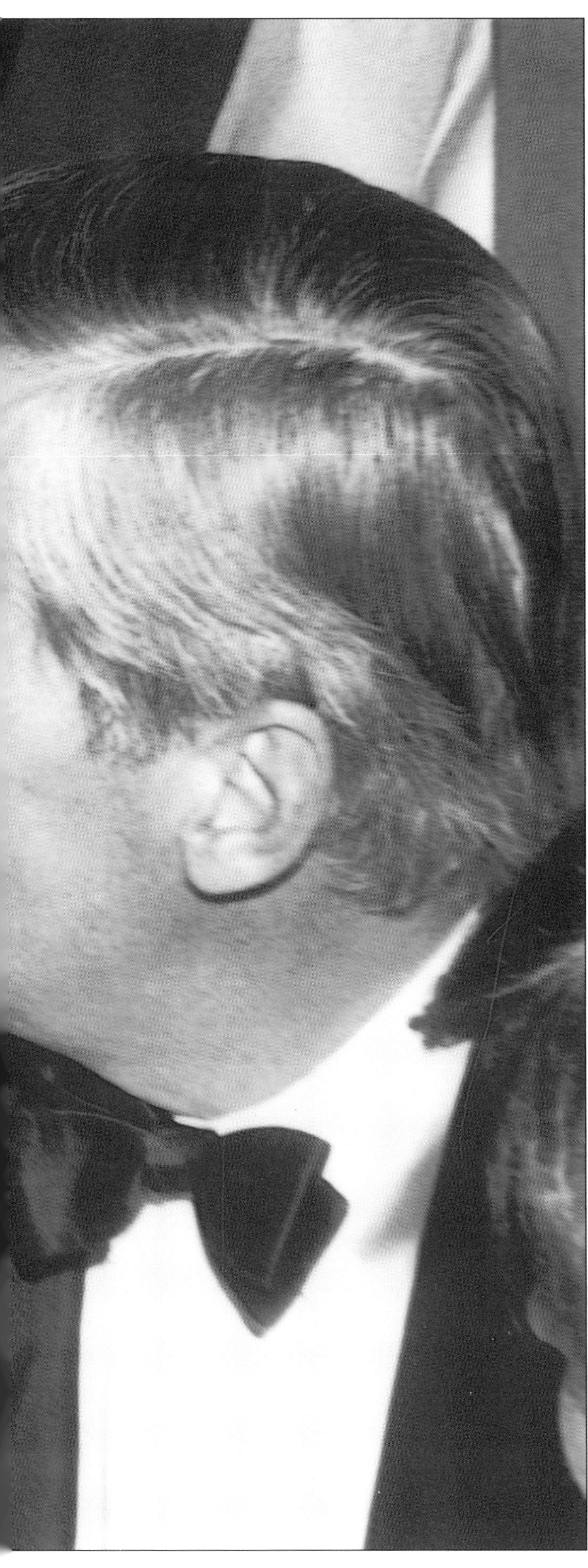

Chapter Twenty-Nine

Doubles has become one of the most popular private clubs in the country and I'm very proud to have been a co-founder. I'll never forget one summer being in Monte Carlo prior to sailing off on Charles Revson's ULTIMA. I had accompanied Eugenia Sheppard to the Hotel de Paris and while waiting for her to file her regular column for the New York *Post,* I was approached by a gentleman who said, "Aren't you Earl Blackwell?" I nodded "yes" and he continued, "I just read about you in *New York Magazine* on the plane coming over." I was surprised for I hadn't seen the article, so he showed it to me. He then asked, "How would you like to make $100,000?" I gulped and this time nodded a big "Yes." He explained that he had taken lease on El Morocco and he wanted me to make it into a private club. I thanked him, but explained I was one of the founders of Raffles and couldn't be involved in two similar projects.

A year later, Joseph Norban (the man I had met in Monte Carlo) called and said, "I've just taken a long lease in the space occupied by Raffles in the Sherry Netherland. Now that Raffles is closed, will you reconsider my offer?" I replied, "For it's success, you must have your own kitchen and not share it with the hotel. Also, you must adhere to rigid rules." I had learned that one of the reasons for the demise of Raffles was that outsiders would give a substantial tip to one of the head waiters and enter the club.

Right now, Joseph Norban's daughter, Wendy, leads everything at Doubles. Today, Porter Ijams is President and under Wendy Carduna's phenomenal supervision, the club is outstanding.

Arlene Dahl & Marc Rosen recently invited 100 friends to celebrate their
7th Wedding Anniversary and chose Doubles as the ideal place for the party.

Martha Stewart and Howard Cushing

Nancy Ittleson & Dennis Stein

Chapter Thirty

Great Harbour Cay is a special paradise to those who have discovered the Island and built their homes here. Usually the first question one is asked by a fellow neighbor is, "How did you first hear of this Island?"

Well, in my case, it was in the late sixties when my good friend, Douglas Fairbanks, Jr., invited me to fly down to see the beautiful Bahamian Island he had recently discovered. The day we arrived the superb 18-hole golf course was officially dedicated but the golf club house was not completed and we had lunch under the palm trees at the airport.

It was love at first sight for me. I returned several times the following year and on one visit brought along Frank and Didi Shields. Their reaction was instant, just as mine had been. Before too long Frank and I dreamed of a very special membership club and with Jim Raymond and Bill Hunt's enthusiasm and support along with John Chase, Tom Pulling, Bill Roosevelt and others we secured property on the Marina and Beach (adjoining the 16th hole) and started construction of the present Club House.

We took the romantic name of TAMBOO from a small row boat that had once belonged to a group of fishermen from Tampa, Florida. They had come to the Island in the late forties and occupied a small house perched on the hill overlooking the entrance to what is now the Marina.

In the early seventies when GREAT HARBOUR CAY was being developed as a resort, a distinguished group of international travelers visited the Island and soon the TAMBOO Club was a favorite gathering place for people like Cary Grant, the Duke of Marlborough, Margot Fonteyn, Walter Cronkite, Curt Jurgens, William Buckley, etc.

Today, GREAT HARBOUR CAY has been maintained as a "private island" for a coterie of island aficionados who recognize and support its unsurpassed charm. The great vision and continued support of Mickey Briggs has helped make the island even more beautiful.

Opposite Page Top:
I enjoy my winter home in the Bahamas, especially when friends like Susan Blakely and Deborah Raffin stop by unexpectedly for lunch.

Opposite Page Middle:
Although I'm only 100 yards from the ocean, I enjoy a couple of swims a day in my 50 ft. pool.

Opposite Page Left:
Pat & Bob Schuler are wonderful houseguests. Even with Pat's active career (she's celebrating her 40th Anniversary at The Met) they always manage to visit.

Opposite Page Right:
With no telephone and very little social life, Eugenia Sheppard and I found my Bahamian home to be the perfect place to write 3 novels.

Pictured here with Lady Frances Peek and Mr. & Mrs. Douglas Fairbanks, Jr.

Miss Phoenix

Chapter Thirty-One

As I think about these concluding pages of the book, Miss Phoenix reminds me, "You better take a nap — you're going out this evening. I'm glad it's not black tie, so you won't be out too late." She then continues, "I've ordered a car. It will be here at 7:30."

That's the way she is, my Miss Phoenix. One in a million. She has organized my professional and personal life for over 35 years. Her constant crack of the whip, coupled with her incomparable care has kept me on my toes.

In 1989, Miss Phoenix made sure my 50th Anniversary Party of Celebrity Service was perfect. She supervised the caterers, addressed the invitations by hand, and impeccably prepared the Ballroom for the party. In her usual style, she double checked that my friends, staff and neighbors all came to this celebration. The unforgettable guest list included: Arlene Dahl & Marc Rosen, Patrice Munsel & Bob Schuler, Liliane Montevecchi, Rose Sachs, Aileen Mehle, Cindy & Joey Adams, Ted Van Antwerp, Max Showalter, George S. Kaufman, Jean Dalrymple, Liz Smith, Iris Love, Pauline Trigere, Budd Calisch, Billy Norwich, Radie Harris, Tammy Grimes, Charles Strouse, Eva Gabor, Rita Gam, Milton Goldman, Ruth Ford, Joe Deva, Michael Sean O'Shea, Estee Lauder, Phyllis Schwartz, Vicki Bagley, Barbara McGurn, Michael & Natalie Sparber, Lucille Lortel, Lady Jean Campbell and the wonderful staff from Celebrity Service (still working at the office today!) Bill Murray, Jeff Kormos, Frank Gehrecke, Frances Van, Carol Schiff and Nancy Preiser.

At the moment, Miss Phoenix is hard at work preparing another big event. On December 2, 1991, the Parkinson's Foundation is honoring me at the Beverly Hills Hotel in California. Betsy Bloomingdale and Nancy Vreeland are chairing the dinner and Gregory Peck is one of the Honorary Chairmen. At the same time, my faithful associate is pursuing donations for the Theater Hall of Fame and organizing the upcoming ballot.

As I said at the very beginning of the book, I've always been fascinated with fame. For over half a century, I have been a keen observer and an active participant of the Celebrity Parade. I never cease to be excited by the emergence of a new "Name." While working closely with Patsy Maharam on this book, I became more aware of the extraordinary musical talents of this adorable young red-head and I have no doubt in my mind she is destined for fame.

I never give up! I was born under the sign of Taurus and I am a fighter. In spite of Parkinson's and my Birthdays that seem to fly by, I continue my special projects.

Summing up an autobiography is not an easy task. I would like to share something my father said to me. *"Never pretend or try to be anything but your own natural self."* It was good advice. I've been around the world a couple of times and dined at Palaces, but I've never outgrown my taste for pecan pie.

For the past few years I've had to curtail some of my activities because of my Parkinson's problem. When President Reagan invited me for a State Dinner at the White House, during his administration, I stood in line, holding onto my cane. Waiting to be presented, I said a silent prayer: "Lord, let me walk straight and meet the President without stumbling." And my prayer was answered.

The day Cary Grant died, I opened my mail to find a copy of Danton Walker's book "Danton's Inferno" along with a personal letter from Cary saying: "Earl, my friend, y'see-it was this way. I was riffling through a pile of old books preparatory to throwing them away when I came across your fine physiognomy illuminating tho' partly covered by Tallulah's profile, a table at some secluded rendezvous, and since I never forget a face, especially a friendly face, I thought, because your looks have changed so very little, you might enjoy a moment's nostalgia. There's no acknowledgment needed. Someday we're sure to find ourselves talking over the telephone or the garden fence. Meanwhile, happy thoughts. Cary."

A rare moment: Louella Parsons and Hedda Hopper together at my Penthouse.

Frank Sinatra dancing with Cyd Charisse

Here's Lucy — (Lucille Ball)

Mary Martin, Gower Champion & Robert Preston

Perle Mesta & Shirley Jones

Larry Hagman with Mom, Mary Martin

Darlin' Earl— Look! I'm so happy to be "75" and still here! To wish you a Merry Christmas— Always Your Lovin' Mary

The whole Drexel Family
(Photo: Jade Albert)

At the Findlay Gallery:
Mr. & Mrs. Joseph H. (Estee) Lauder,
Mrs. T. Suffern (Jean) Tailer and
Mr. & Mrs. Cornelius V. Whitney.
(Photo credit: Bert & Richard Morgan Studio)

Mr. & Mrs. Thomas Pulling

John Kluge with John II

My sister Mary, on a visit to me in California; Summer 1936.

*My aunt, Bernice Blackwell Davidson,
lunching with Vivian Wowlley-Hart at the Stonehenge.*

I love music and how fortunate I was to have been invited to the Metropolitan Opera for 2 or 3 times a week. One of my hosts was George deCuevas and his wife Margaret (the daughter of John D. Rockefeller); another was my beloved Godmother, Mother Terry.

Mother Terry had one of the large center boxes and she would fill it with friends every Monday night. In those days, opening night at the Opera was the most glamorous event of the year. Limousines lined 39th street and there were at least 100 photographers. Every socialite attended the event.

When my sister, Mary, unexpectedly came to New York for a visit, Mother Terry telephoned to apologize that her box was full and couldn't include her, too. A few hours later, she re-called, happy that a seat had become available and she wanted Mary to attend. As Mary and I entered the box, we noticed an attractive elderly lady, right next to Mother Terry. She was leaning over the rail, arms outstretched, pretending to lead the orchestra. Mary gave me a quizzical look as if to say: "This is New York? Top Society?"

During intermission, we all walked to Sherrys where we had a reserved table. As I had a glass of champagne, I realized it was obvious that the lady in question already had quite a few glasses before she arrived.

A photographer approached our table and started snapping. To my astonishment, the lady thumbed-her-nose at the cameraman. The next day the photograph appeared in both the *Daily News* and *Mirror* with the caption: "Who was the lady thumbing-her-nose at the Opera?" The lady, Mrs. Henry L. Dougherty, was so embarrassed that she contributed $500,000 to the Opera fund.

Mary Lasker

Tommy Tune with Gina Lollobrigida

Lillian Emerson

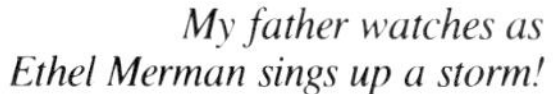

*My father watches as
Ethel Merman sings up a storm!*

*Sharing a wonderful evening (left to right):
Designer Valentino, Ruth Ford, Liza, Jack Haley, Jr.,
Margaux Hemingway & her husband Errol Weston.*

*Jack Haley, Jr. & Liza Minnelli
captured during a quiet moment in my ballroom.*

Dorothy Strelsin & Laurence Harvey

*Dorothy Strelsin bought her California home from Laurence Harvey
and I have the pleasure, each Summer to sleep in his bed.
I first met Laurence Harvey at the Venice Film Festival of 1953
and became good friends when he appeared on Broadway in 1957
in "The Country Wife."*

With Jerry Zipkin in Rome.

At the Stork Club with Celeste Holm (left) and Joan Bennett (right)

Dining out with John Bruno (left) the owner of Pen & Pencil are Judy Garland & husband Sid Luft.

Judy Garland puckers up to Charles Walters who directed her in 'Easter Parade.''

Edgar Lansbury and Ingrid Bergman

Francis X Bushman and Cliff Robertson

Dining out at the El Morocco
with Frank Hale (Palm Beach
Playhouse)
and Irene Dunne.

At the Cincetta Studios in Rome
shooting "A MATTER OF TIME"
are left to right: The Marquis
Raymundo de Larraine, Charles
Boyer, Earl Blackwell and Academy
Award Winning Director Vincente
Minnelli

Celebrating the publication of
"Celebrity Register": (left to right)
Cleveland Amory, Perle Mesta,
Salvador Dali and Joan Crawford.

Joan Crawford greets Ethel
Merman and Russell Nype
with a warm hello!

with Joan Crawford

"The Hostess
With The Mostest"
Perle Mesta

Carol Channing is the center
of attention at a party I
threw for her. Pictured here
with Tallulah Bankhead
(right) and Natalie Wood
(center) while discussing
diamonds!

At The Harwyn, Joan Crawford
steps up to the mike to introduce
Eddie Fisher.

Katharine Hepburn leaving the famous London Clinic to have a dressing put on a cut finger. She was in London to play "The Lion In Winter" opposite Peter O'Toole.

With Sophia Loren

My good friend, Nancy Cooke Jackson De Herrara visits with the Maharishi in India with some very famous followers: Mia Farrow, Nancy Cooke Jackson De Herrara, John Lennon & George Harrison

In 1954 with Norma Shearer & Cole Porter (Photo: Edward Ozern)

Mary Lou Whitney and Budd Calisch

(Inset) *Young Brooke with her Mom, Teri.*

with Brooke Shields

DESTINED FOR FAME

Many years ago, I started collecting photographs of friends taken when they were children. They all appear in this book.

How many can you identify?

See page 162 for answers.

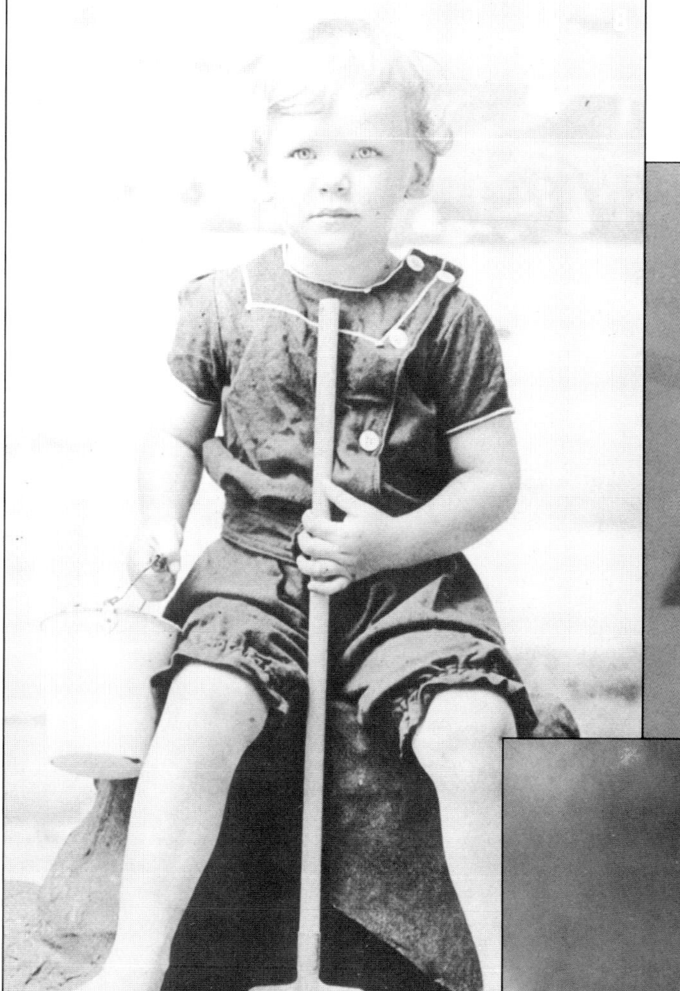

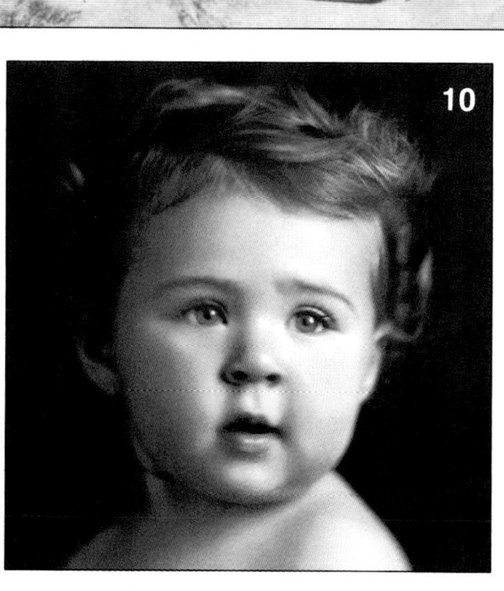

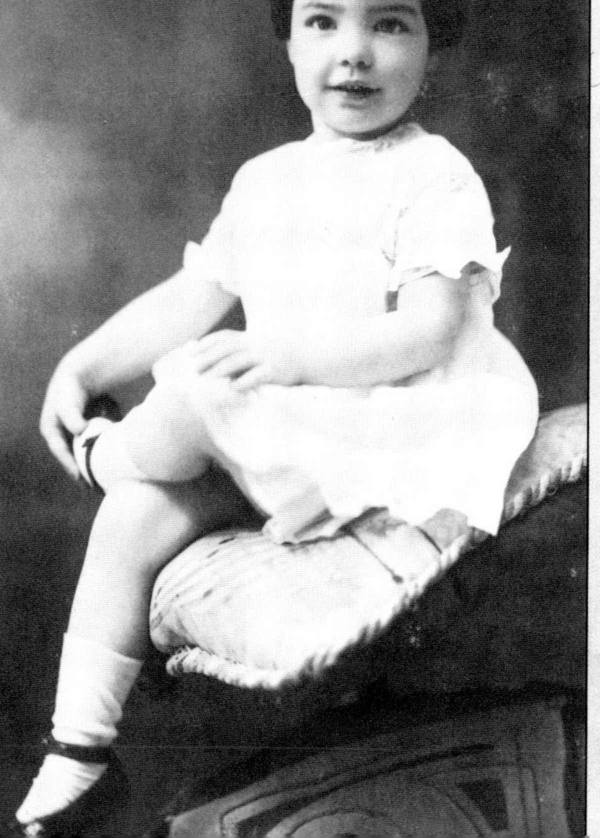

Answers for DESTINED FOR FAME, pp. 156-157

1. Henry Fonda   2. The Gabors (left to right: Eva, Zsa Zsa and Magda)   3. Hugh O'Brian   4. Joan Crawford   5. Suzy (Aileen Mehle)
6. Eugenia Sheppard 7. Gloria Vanderbilt 8. Douglas Fairbanks, Jr. 9. Lucille Lortel 10. Betsy Bloomingdale 11. Ruth Ford 12. Diana Vreeland